# Pharmaceutical
# Price Regulation

# Pharmaceutical Price Regulation

## Public Perceptions, Economic Realities, and Empirical Evidence

John A. Vernon
and
Joseph H. Golec

The AEI Press

*Publisher for the American Enterprise Institute*

WASHINGTON, D.C.

To order call toll free 1-800-462-6420 or 1-717-794-3800. For all other inquiries please contact the AEI Press, 1150 Seventeenth Street, N.W., Washington, D.C. 20036 or call 1-800-862-5801.

 **NRI** NATIONAL RESEARCH INITIATIVE

This publication is a project of the National Research Initiative, a program of the American Enterprise Institute that is designed to support, publish, and disseminate research by university-based scholars and other independent researchers who are engaged in the exploration of important public policy issues.

Library of Congress Cataloging-in-Publication Data

Vernon, John A.
Pharmaceutical price regulation : public perceptions, economic
realities, and empirical evidence / John A. Vernon and Joseph H. Golec.
    p. ; cm.
Includes bibliographical references.
    ISBN-13: 978-0-8447-4277-9
    ISBN-10: 0-8447-4277-5
1. Pharmaceutical industry—Government policy—United States.
2. Drugs—Prices—Law and legislation—United States. I. Golec, Joseph.
II. Title.

    HD9666.6.V47 2008
    338.4'361510973--dc22

                                                            2008049681

12 11 10 09        1 2 3 4 5

# Contents

# List of Illustrations

# Introduction

Over the past forty years, pharmaceutical innovation has saved countless lives and improved the quality of life for millions of people. Although these benefits are enormous, the costs of developing breakthrough medicines are staggering, and rarely appreciated. The average cost of bringing a single new drug to the marketplace—covering years or even decades of research and development, safety tests, clinical trials, and regulatory approval—is about $1 billion (DiMasi, Hansen, and Grabowski 2003). The process isn't just expensive, it's risky. For every blockbuster drug, dozens of other drugs fail to earn back their upfront investment.

What propels the pharmaceutical industry to keep taking these risks? It is the expectation that as physicians and consumers embrace the new medicines, the drug companies themselves will be able to make enough profit over time to justify their expensive effort.

Unfortunately, today drug development is under siege, both around the world and, increasingly, in the United States. The large profits earned on a relatively small number of successful, high-priced medicines have created a clamor for government-imposed price controls. At least ten developed countries control "launch" prices on new drugs. At least sixteen countries control reimbursement prices. Moreover, most of Western Europe, Canada, Australia, and New Zealand have imposed a system of indirect controls by requiring cost-effectiveness analysis (CEA) before approving payment for a drug. The United Kingdom has perhaps the most stringent form of CEA; it recently refused to pay for Alzheimer's drugs in all but the most severe cases, triggering a patient backlash.

So far, the U.S. Medicare program has not adopted a similar policy

1

(Neumann, Rosen, and Weinstein 2005). Doing so would be widely unpopular. Yet the Centers for Medicare and Medicaid Services (CMS) could soon yield to budget pressures from the new Medicare drug benefit and start formalizing reimbursement decisions using CEA methods. In 2006, the influential Institute of Medicine released guidelines (at the request of the U.S. Office of Management and Budget) on how best to implement and conduct these analyses (Miller, Robinson, and Lawrence 2006).

Regulators have questioned some drugs' effectiveness in treating life-threatening diseases, especially given their sky-high prices. In 2007 and again in 2008, the Food and Drug Administration (FDA) expressed concerns about Aranesp and Epogen, developed by Amgen, and Procrit, developed by Johnson & Johnson. Separately, members of Congress criticized the companies for aggressive marketing of the drugs. These drugs, used to treat anemia caused by kidney disease or chemotherapy, had combined sales of $10 billion in 2006 and were the single biggest drug expense for Medicare (Berenson and Pollack 2007).

Controversy swirls around pricing of some of the most high-profile, high-priced breakthrough drugs that have emerged from big-budget, high-risk R&D efforts. Look, for instance, at Genentech Inc.'s Avastin. Used to treat colorectal, lung, and other cancers, Avastin can cost $55,000 or more for a year's supply. Genentech is under increasing pressure from Congress and Medicare to curb prices, but Genentech's chief executive argues that the company must charge premiums on Avastin and other successful anticancer drugs to recoup the company's $1.8 billion annual R&D budget (Chase 2007).

Indirect forms of price controls are already on the rise across the United States, as exemplified by the ongoing controversy over legalized drug importation. Bills are pending in Congress that would legalize reimportation of pharmaceuticals nationally. As we will argue, allowing drug reimportation is a frontal assault on the future of pharmaceutical industry R&D. Drug importation undermines drug companies' efforts to charge different prices in different markets. This erosion of competition leads to a single worldwide price, one that is simultaneously too high for many poorer countries and too low for drug companies seeking to recoup their upfront R&D investments.

Advocates in the United States and abroad believe that direct or indirect price controls such as CEA and drug reimportation can provide a free lunch. In their view, pharmaceutical companies can charge lower prices and still make enough profit to encourage them to develop future innovative medicines. Unfortunately, these advocates, as well as a large segment of the American public, have failed to grasp the connection between the temporarily high prices paid for new drugs and the level of R&D that takes place inside pharmaceutical and biotechnology companies. A random sampling of 1,006 Americans surveyed in 2005 indicated a telling lack of knowledge about the pharmaceutical R&D process:[1]

- Only 40 percent of the respondents believed that if the government controlled drug prices, R&D spending would drop. Nearly half said spending would be unchanged, and 15 percent thought it would rise.

- Only 27 percent of the respondents believed that allowing drug importation from Canada would result in a drop in R&D expenditure. Moreover, 48 percent "strongly" disagreed that importation would hurt research.

- Nevertheless, the survey turned up strong evidence that Americans want pharmaceutical R&D to continue. Given a choice between lower prices on existing drugs and continued R&D, 55 percent voted for continued research and only 36 percent favored lower costs.

This monograph will argue that pharmaceutical price controls constitute a short-sighted, wrong-headed, and possibly dangerous policy. The prices set by the free market are the signals that corporations need in order to decide whether to undertake expensive, risky research into new drugs. Free-market pricing is essentially a voting mechanism, whereby consumers can send signals to producers about what they value.

As we will argue, there is an unmistakable historical connection between price controls and lower levels of drug R&D. By extension, price controls ultimately lead to the introduction of fewer new, and potentially life-saving, medicines. In short, there is no free lunch in drug pricing. Pharmaceutical price regulations reduce pharmaceutical R&D spending, and this monograph will demonstrate the fallacy of believing otherwise.

Europe's experience with price controls is one proof of our point. The European Union (EU) has largely controlled prices, and R&D spending has dropped as a result. Between 1985 and 2004, the European Union's price controls resulted in a near-zero drug inflation rate, with a cumulative 4 percent increase in prices over a twenty-year period (Golec and Vernon 2006). But this tight control over drug spending led to very sharp restraints on drug R&D spending. In the mid-1980s, Europe's drug R&D spending exceeded that of the United States by 24 percent. But since 1986, Europe's pharmaceutical industry R&D has grown at merely one half the rate of America's. By 2004, Europe's spending trailed U.S. spending by 15 percent.[2]

This reversal occurred at a time when U.S. drug prices rose by 51 percent, when U.S. firms' profit margins far exceeded those of EU firms, and when stock market returns of U.S. pharmaceutical companies were double those of their European counterparts. These are, we argue, the key ingredients of a robust R&D culture. Our models over this time horizon suggest that EU-type price controls in the United States would have led to a decline of about 40 percent in R&D spending over that eighteen-year span.

This monograph will also show that America's mere flirtation with strict government price controls—the Clinton health plan of 1993—took a heavy toll on the very companies that conduct the most intensive R&D into new drugs. Our research into the stock market effects of the Clinton plan shows that the more intensely R&D-focused a drug company, the more its stocks dropped in the aftermath of the plan's announcement. Small biotechnology firms' stock prices fell the most, and recovered only slowly.

Our strong contention is that the U.S. pharmaceutical market is relatively free and has worked reasonably well. For example, the early success (and profits) of Merck's Mevacor led to the introduction of other statins such as Merck's Zocor, Bristol-Myers Squibb's Provachol, Pfizer's Lipitor, AstraZeneca's Crestor, and Schering-Plough's Zetia. Each drug represents an advance, and through price and sales, the producer and the consumer signal one another about just how advanced and useful it is, and how desired.

Critics argue that drug companies invest billions of dollars in frivolous "lifestyle" drugs. Even if this is so, it raises a valuable question: what kinds of drug development would likely be starved by price controls? Our evidence suggests that it would *not* be the so-called lifestyle drugs that would suffer, but instead life-saving drugs, such as Gleevec (for the treatment of leukemia), because they tend to be higher priced.

Some believe that free-market prices do not work well for pharmaceuticals because consumers cannot properly judge the value of complex, high-technology goods. But consumers often rely on experts (e.g., financial advisers, lawyers, consultants) to help them to judge the effectiveness of many complex goods in areas where they lack expertise. For pharmaceuticals, consumers rely on physicians and pharmacists, and even trusted health care Web sites such as WebMD.

Free-market prices certainly work quite well for many other high-tech products. For example, consumers signaled to all potential producers of mobile communications devices that they were willing to pay a high price (and support high profits) for a device like the Blackberry Smartphone. Blackberry maintained its relatively high price until a better product (iPhone) came along. Blackberry's response to the emergence of a superior product has been to lower its own price.

It is possible to object that the market for drugs differs from the market for mobile communications devices. Consumers in the latter market may accept high prices, which signal high value and often exclusivity—that is, only those willing and able to pay the price may possess the good. Unlike iPhones, however, health care is often regarded as a necessity rather than a luxury, a basic human entitlement that should be available to all at a "fair" (i.e., government-controlled) price.

But this argument fails to consider that even low-priced, generic drugs rely on unrestricted budgets for pharmaceutical R&D. Without initial high prices to cover large R&D costs, few new breakthroughs would be forthcoming. Fewer competitor medicines would follow at lower prices, and fewer cheap generics would follow these. The virtuous cycle of R&D spending, innovation, and competition grinds to a halt when governments constrain prices, because low initial prices mean investors will not earn the high return required to encourage high-risk R&D investment.

Lastly, it's worth mentioning that in the United States, some areas of drug R&D, such as vaccines, have been largely abandoned by big pharmaceutical companies—at least partly because the U.S. government, as the sole or most important buyer, has insisted on paying rock-bottom prices. Friedrich Hayek (1945) eloquently explained long ago why free market prices are the best mechanisms for determining production and consumption. Alternative social mechanisms have failed time and again. Yet an effort is afoot to replace the free market with the wisdom of government bureaucrats.

These bureaucrats want to measure how much more effective one drug is than another, and how much the incremental effectiveness is worth in terms of price. Drugs judged to be breakthroughs will get the "right" price that will encourage future breakthroughs. In other words, government controls propose to better the market through product-information aggregation, consumer-benefit measurement, and relative pricing.

Another effort to improve on the free market would have the government "negotiate" a free-market price with pharmaceutical producers, because it pays a large fraction of the pharmaceutical bill. But government negotiation is likely to become government dictation, as prices reflect political forces such as government budgets. With continuously tight budgets, prices offered by the government may no longer reflect the value of a medicine's effectiveness but instead reflect budget demands to reduce expenses. The short-run benefit is lower prices, but the long-run costs are fewer new medicines for current and future generations.

As health care rises to the top of the national agenda in the United States, and with fiscal budget deficits growing, drug pricing will soon likely emerge as a vital issue for policymakers. It is alarming to us that so few American consumers can at this crucial stage envision the disturbing consequences of government price controls for new drugs. Few American consumers understand the value of initial high drug prices. Even sophisticated consumers don't see the connection between prices, R&D spending, and new drugs.

Chapter 1 lays out a model of how drug companies decide to move forward with drug development, pointing out that even after launch, only about 30 percent of new drugs eventually earn back their investments. This chapter also shows the many factors that increase the cost and risk of new drug launches. Among them are the delays in product launch that occur as companies and governments haggle over prices.

Chapter 2 explains the effects of financial incentives and government price setting on the level of pharmaceutical R&D spending and the introduction of new medicines. Budget-constrained governments are likely to show a bias toward low-priced, low-value pharmaceuticals as opposed to high-priced, high-value ones. This is unlikely to be corrected through voting, especially in the short run, because the benefits of current lower prices are easy to see, while the costs of forgone future medicines are not.

There is little doubt that consumers need some intermediary to guide them in their decisions about which pharmaceuticals are best for them. But there is little reason to believe that consumers should rely on government bureaucrats to represent their interests properly in selecting pharmaceuticals. This is because bureaucrats' incentives are driven by the exigencies of budgets and not by the needs of consumers.

Chapter 3 discusses the artificial mechanisms employed by some government bureaucracies to select among pharmaceuticals and to rationalize price controls. Although some are quite technical they are unlikely to produce optimal results. This is because governments often succumb to short-term political fixes, i.e., lower prices today. Budget constraints have led many policymakers to adopt a goal of zero real pharmaceutical price inflation, without any economic rationale for why prices for superior goods like pharmaceuticals should exhibit no real increase.

Chapter 4 offers a summary of our conclusions and makes recommendations. We oppose legislation that would permit large-scale or wholesale drug reimportation. We urge the Centers for Medicare and Medicaid to refrain from imposing European-style price controls on—or applying cost-effectiveness analysis to—drugs administered under their programs.

We believe that the present system of drug pricing in the United States works quite well. Despite its flaws, it is better than any other in existence in countries with single-payer (i.e., government) systems. Some of these countries enjoy lower drug prices, but the trade-off is rationing, a paucity of development, and poor market signals about what's valued by patients and their doctors. Above all, we conclude that all too often, governments and voters choose short-term gains, in the form of lower prices, while ignoring the great long-term benefits that flow from temporarily higher prices and profits.

# 1

## R&D Investment in New Drugs: How It Works, and How It Is Harmed by Price Controls

In this chapter, we will explain how pharmaceutical companies make their investment decisions. We will put forth a detailed model of how executives make a series of "go/no-go" decisions regarding expensive drug development. We will then show how government price controls tilt the decision toward the negative, reducing drug companies' incentive to decide "go" and putting in place obstacles that make it more compelling to decide "no go."

In the final section of the chapter, we will demonstrate that this model of corporate R&D investment is based on long-term payoffs. As such, it is vulnerable to attack from politicians and voters, who often prefer short-term gains in the form of immediate lower prices, not fully understanding how this imperils the long-term goal of getting better drugs in the future.

In many respects, drug development is similar to the wildcatter's search for oil, with its many dry holes and uncertainty. Drug "prospecting" is an arduous task, involving long development times, high costs, and low probabilities of technical success. Before an investigational new compound ultimately reaches the market, it must advance through several stages of research and clinical development: preclinical testing in animals and three phases of successful clinical testing in humans. It must then receive FDA approval. This process is heavily regulated, and attrition rates are high. On average, only one out of several thousand investigational compounds goes on to become a marketed drug. The vast majority fail

FIGURE 1-1

THE DRUG DEVELOPMENT PROCESS

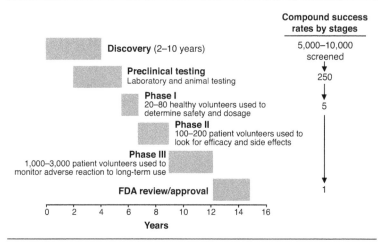

SOURCE: PhRMA, based on data from Center for the Study of Drug Development, Tufts University, 1995.

at some point in the development process, whether because of safety concerns, or because the compound doesn't work as well as hoped, or because the prospects for profitability are too low. The average length of time from discovery to market launch is approximately fifteen years (DiMasi, Hansen, and Grabowski 2003). The pharmaceutical R&D process is illustrated in figure 1-1.

On average, firms must invest in many unsuccessful R&D projects before they find a successful one; that results in a marketed product. The costs associated with failed R&D projects are thus unavoidable and must be factored into the average cost of drug development. One recent estimate places this cost on a pretax basis at $802 million per FDA-approved drug (new chemical entity) in year 2000 dollars (DiMasi, Hansen, and Grabowski 2003), although both higher and lower estimates exist. On an after-tax basis, assuming the firm has sufficient revenues to capture the tax benefits of R&D, or is in a position to sell these tax benefits, the estimated cost of developing an average drug is $480 million (Grabowski, Vernon, and DiMasi 2002).

It is important to emphasize that these figures don't simply measure the cost of drugs that become successes in the marketplace. They factor in, as they should, the cost of failures, as well as the cost of developing drugs that ultimately reach the marketplace but never earn back their initial development costs.

In fact, only three out of ten marketed drugs earn back their investments. Because the decision to market a drug is made after R&D costs are incurred, some drugs are marketed despite being unprofitable. Having already sunk many millions of dollars into development, drug companies often decide it is better to earn low revenue rather than kill the product and get zero revenue. Usually, drug companies take this course if their expected revenue will exceed the marginal cost of merely producing and selling the drug, after the R&D phase.

As figure 1-2 shows, the best-selling drugs—the top 10 percent of new drugs by sales—earn back their investment several times over. The next 20 percent also do fairly well, as their cumulative revenue over time is greater than the cumulative cost. But the bottom 70 percent fail to clear the bar, i.e., the cost of developing one of these drugs exceeds its total sales over the life of the drug. And of course, in many of these cases, the R&D money is spent but the drug never makes it to market, so the revenue is zero.

Figure 1-2 presents the skewed nature of revenues in pharmaceutical R&D. It assumes that the after-tax costs are fixed at $480 million, although they could be skewed as well.

Average net revenues adjusted for time value over all deciles is estimated to be $525 million, after taxes. At the time of product launch, the average economic value of pharmaceutical research and development activities is approximately $45 million ($525 – $480). This value is what provides incentives for investment in the pharmaceutical industry, and under current conditions it appears that, on average, there is an incentive for continued investment.

In a sense, this is good news. The pharmaceutical success stories more than compensate for the duds. Overall, then, it is rational for the drug industry to invest in R&D, because it recoups its costs, although not by the fantastic margins that some critics claim.

FIGURE 1-2

SKEWED DISTRIBUTION OF R&D PROJECT REVENUES

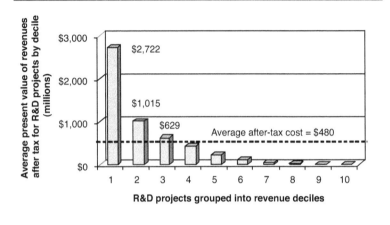

SOURCE: Grabowski et al., *PharmacoEconomics*, vol. 20, supplement 3, 2002.

The trouble, as we show in detail below, is that price regulation creates fewer potential "winners."

### Conceptual Model and Theory of Price Regulation

Let's focus our attention on the first critical decision point in the life of a pharmaceutical product's development, the time of the Phase I "go/no-go" decision. This is the point at which a firm decides if a compound it has been studying in laboratories is ready for testing in humans. At this stage, all in vitro (test tube) and animal tests have been completed, the mechanism of action is reasonably well understood, and there is a general belief that the compound's medical benefits outweigh its risks in addressing a specific ailment. It is also at this point that the first financial modeling of the compound's commercial potential is conducted.

We'll use the net present value approach, which calculates investment return, in a somewhat simplified version, as follows: First, a company takes the sum of all expected future revenue from the drug.

Then, it calculates the accumulated costs, all the while adjusting for the fact that the company is deploying, over time, capital that carries a cost. Specifically, firms often fund R&D by selling stock to investors, who expect to earn a return that exceeds the return on a bond from the same company. While pharmaceutical companies seldom issue new bonds to finance their R&D projects, the required returns on stocks are analogous to the interest payments on bonds (only they come from stock price appreciation and dividends). A common practice is to include the returns required by investors on the capital that funds R&D, up until the year of FDA approval. This "capitalized" value, which incorporates expenditures on both successful and failed R&D projects, represents the true economic cost of bringing a new drug to market.

To move ahead with a drug, companies need to project that their accumulated sales will exceed their total costs, making sure to adjust for their own costs of funds over these years. Thus the firm makes the Phase I "go/no-go" decision by first calculating expected cash flows year by year—i.e., the difference between the cash revenues and production expenses expected in each year over the period of time when the drug will be marketed. These can be positive or negative, but we assume here that they are positive. We also assume FDA approval. Next, the cost of clinical trials is computed for each year until the point of FDA approval. These are all negative cash flows. Finally, the negative clinical cash flows are weighed against the positive net cash flows from future sales. But the cash flows are not simply added together, because each comes in a different year, and the value of a dollar in later years is smaller than in earlier years. Therefore, each cash flow is adjusted for time value. The time-value adjustment depends upon a firm's cost of stock and/or bond financing. The adjusted figures are summed together to produce a net present value, which, if positive, implies that the particular drug project is a "go." If negative, it's a "no-go."[1]

Now let's look at the effect of price controls. If government imposes a reduction in the price of a drug, overall revenues will very likely decline, as numerous studies have demonstrated that the demand for drugs is inelastic (Coulson and Stuart 1995; Santerre

FIGURE 1-3

## THE EFFECT OF PHARMACEUTICAL PRICE REGULATION ON CASH FLOWS

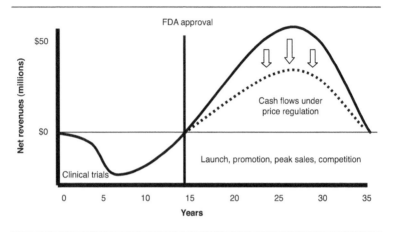

SOURCE: Adapted from Robert Helms, "The Impact of Pharmaceutical Price Controls on R&D," presentation, AEI-Brookings Joint Center for Regulatory Studies, May 16, 2005, http://www. aei.org/publications/filter.all,pubID.22650/pub_detail.asp.

and Vernon 2006). That is, price drops won't create a big rise in sales volume to produce a rise in overall revenue

Figure 1-3 illustrates how revenue declines in a government price-control scenario but the costs of clinical development do not. Clearly, the negative cash flows associated with clinical development do not change, while the positive expected future cash flows from sales fall significantly. If the positive expected future cash flows fall enough so that the total of positive cash flows no longer exceeds the total of negative clinical cash flows (after time-value adjustment), then the drug will not proceed into clinical trials.

Price regulation can have additional negative effects. Danzon, Wang, and Wang (2003) have shown that pharmaceutical price regulation often results in product launch delays due to government price negotiations. Launch delays would have the effect of shifting the dashed line in figure 1-3 to the right and truncating the period of peak sales by shortening the market exclusivity period.

FIGURE 1-4

THE EFFECT OF PRICE REGULATION ON A FIRM'S INTERNAL RATE
OF RETURN (IRR) AND NUMBER OF R&D PROJECTS

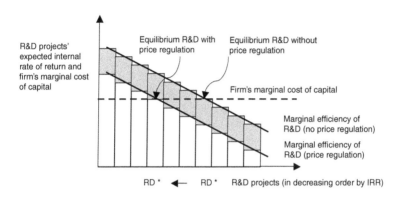

SOURCE: Authors' diagram.

Credible threats of new price regulation will have similar effects (Golec, Hegde, and Vernon 2008). Firms must predict expected cash flows over many years; hence, they must consider the possibility that they will be forced to sell at regulated prices in the future, even if prices are not currently regulated. In other words, the percentage return a firm can expect to earn on its investors' capital (its internal rates of return) will drop under the threat of price regulation, thereby reducing the equilibrium level of R&D investment. This is illustrated in figure 1-4, where the gray boxes reflect the difference between a project's internal rate of return with and without price regulation and RD* is the firm's profit-maximizing level of R&D spending.

Figure 1-4 demonstrates that fewer R&D projects make financial sense under price controls. As prices and expected revenues drop (the slanted lines), fewer and fewer projects will be profitable. Firms will undertake the high return projects first (the vertical bars on the left-hand side of the chart)—and continue to undertake additional investment projects so long as the expected rate of return from the next project exceeds the firm's marginal cost of capital, meaning that fewer of the projects further to the right will pay off. This is the classic supply and demand framework.

In economic terms, price regulation shifts the marginal internal rate of return schedule down, and fewer R&D projects meet the criterion of earning an internal rate of return that exceeds the cost of capital required to fund the project. Investors will not supply capital to fund the marginal projects whose internal rates of return fall below their required returns. These marginal projects could be minor medical advances or major breakthrough medicines. If one assumes that breakthrough medicines can command higher market prices, then price regulation is more likely to be applied to them. Indeed, the Clinton administration's Health Security Act proposed to regulate mostly high-priced breakthrough drugs. After all, there is little cost savings in constraining low-priced, seldom-used drugs.

Finally, figure 1-4 excludes the effects that internal cash flows have on capital supply to the firm. Cash flows exert a positive influence on the level of firm investment spending, but price regulation constrains this internal capital supply and thus reduces R&D investment.

Unfortunately, public debate on this issue can become problematic because firms sometimes proceed with drug development even though they will never earn back their total sunk costs. For many years, the mantra of some industry supporters was that pharmaceutical prices had to be "high" in order to recoup the high fixed costs of R&D. Not true. Firm managers are forward looking and seek to maximize profits; at the time of product launch, R&D costs are sunk and are irrelevant to the calculus of price determination. That is, once a drug reaches the market, its R&D costs have already been incurred and variable costs are the only costs relevant for decision making. Of course, in the long run, if a firm cannot cover its fixed costs, it will go out of business.

Even in cases where the new product is a financial success, the economically efficient and socially optimal market outcome is achieved through fierce competition in the product market, because this drives price down to marginal cost (in the case of perfect competition). However, precisely to the extent that competition achieves these efficiency gains, the economic incentives to invest in research for future technologies are diminished.

But the point here—and it's a vital one—is that drug companies take a long-term view toward investment in R&D and its payoff in the form of revenue and profit. (Paradoxically, these same companies are often characterized as short-sighted and self-serving, when in fact their interests are aligned with the interests of many current and future consumers.) This long-term orientation puts them in conflict with politicians, who serve current voters and their immediate concerns. These politicians speak, all too often, to short-term interests. If the interests of future voters were to be taken into account, government policy might be more evenhanded. However, prices set in the political arena will reflect current voters' wishes, as opposed to the full economic value that pharmaceuticals would attain in a free market.

Striking the optimal balance between the long-run benefits of future innovations and the short-run benefits of patient access to existing medicines is as difficult as it is important. This is due in large part to the fact that future medicines are not observable and are difficult to approximate. This difficulty in estimating long-run benefits may bias the emphasis toward short-run economic interests, which are tangible, straightforward to measure, and easy to grasp.[2] Political agendas of special interest groups are often advanced by false premises and flawed economic logic because it is easier to operate, intentionally or unintentionally, amid a backdrop of public confusion and economic illiteracy.

Figure 1-5 depicts the pharmaceutical trade-off society faces between current and future goods. A new price-control or importation policy (depending on its effectiveness in lowering average drug prices in the United States and the degree of influence of regulated foreign drug prices) will result in a movement from point A to point B. Society gives up some innovation in exchange for improved access to drugs already on the market. Yet the existence of this fundamental trade-off and economic reality has effectively, if not explicitly, been denied by Congress.[3]

FIGURE 1-5
### THE TRADE-OFF BETWEEN ACCESS TO EXISTING MEDICINES AND ACCESS TO FUTURE MEDICINES

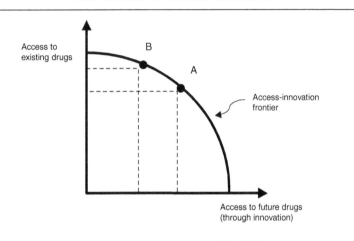

SOURCE: Authors' diagram.

## The Challenge: Addressing the Real Issues

It is difficult to debate the merits of a new policy that shifts the balance between short- and long-run economic efficiency if both parties to the debate and the architects of the policy deny the very existence of this economic reality. The pharmaceutical industry's image problem has no doubt been exacerbated by the prevalence of economic illiteracy in the United States. This illiteracy is manifest in a political process that is messy and imprecise, so that the costs and benefits of alternative policies are often not fully valued. As we will argue, failure to fully measure the costs of pharmaceutical price controls may have a dire effect on future medical innovation.

# 2

# Government Price Regulation and the Impact on Pharmaceutical R&D Spending

Governments around the world have developed many methods for controlling pharmaceutical prices. Some are direct; others are indirect. The effect of these policies has been striking. The EU in particular has succeeded in keeping the rise in drug prices down to the rate of inflation. That stands in sharp contrast to the experience in the United States, where price controls have been almost absent, and where real prices grew about 47 percent faster than EU pharmaceutical prices between 1985 and 2004 (Golec and Vernon 2006).

The bulk of this chapter will examine how these starkly different levels of drug pricing have led to equally striking differences in the levels of pharmaceutical R&D spending. As we will demonstrate, European drug R&D has fallen far behind levels in the United States. Where once Europe was a leader, it has in the past two decades become a notable drug-research laggard. Our research will show that there is more than merely a link between price controls and diminished R&D, but a compelling cause and effect relationship. That is, government controls that keep prices down also keep drug R&D down. By contrast, the dominance of free-market pricing in the United States has led to robust spending on drug R&D over the past twenty years.

We can study the effect of regulated prices on pharmaceutical R&D spending using three approaches. First, we can simply look at correlations between average industry prices and industry R&D over time. Second, we can explore the connection between changes in prices and profits on the one hand and R&D spending on the other. Finally, we can show how price controls affect firms' stock prices, and then how stock prices influence R&D decisions. We argue below that because firms sometimes issue stock to finance R&D, lower stock prices result in lower R&D spending.

These different approaches point to the same conclusion: pharmaceutical price regulations reduce pharmaceutical R&D spending. We will offer evidence to support all three conclusions: lower prices, lower profits, and lower stock market valuations all create strong disincentives for drug companies to spend heavily on R&D.

We will also show that if the United States had adopted EU-type price controls, R&D spending in the United States would have been between 24 percent and 40 percent less during the period from 1980 to 2001—causing large but immeasurable harm, as fewer new medicines would have been developed.

### Pharmaceutical Price Regulation and Real Pharmaceutical Price Inflation

Vernon (2003a) catalogues how methods of pharmaceutical price regulation vary from country to country. Table 2-1 provides a list of countries and the various methods they use. The most common methods of controlling pharmaceutical prices are setting rates at which governments reimburse health care providers, and compiling formulary lists of drugs to be dispensed to patients. Directly setting launch prices for medicines is also common. Note that all of the countries use more than one method. Multiple methods may afford them flexibility to fine-tune prices.

Controlling launch prices is a direct form of price setting. Using "reference" prices—that is, fixed prices based on the lowest prices already being paid by a comparison group—often has the same effect. The comparison price may be that of another price-regulated country, usually one where prices are already low. Controlling reimbursement prices or capping doctors' drug budgets theoretically allows consumers to pay more, or doctors to prescribe higher-priced medicines, but the indirect effect of this approach is to constrain

TABLE 2-1
METHODS OF PHARMACEUTICAL PRICE REGULATION BY COUNTRY

| Country | Controls launch prices | Controls reimbursement prices | Uses reference prices | Caps profit rates | Uses positive/ negative listings | Caps doctors' drug budgets |
|---|---|---|---|---|---|---|
| Austria | Yes | Yes | | | Yes | |
| Belgium | Yes | Yes | | | Yes | |
| Canada | Yes | Yes | Yes | | Yes | |
| Denmark | | | Yes | | Yes | |
| Finland | | Yes | | | Yes | |
| France | Yes | Yes | | | Yes | Yes |
| Germany | | Yes | Yes | | Yes | Yes |
| Greece | Yes | Yes | | | Yes | |
| Ireland | Yes | Yes | | | Yes | Yes |
| Italy | Yes | Yes | | | Yes | |
| Japan | | Yes | | Yes | Yes | |
| Netherlands | Yes | Yes | Yes | | Yes | |
| Norway | | Yes | Yes | | Yes | |
| Portugal | Yes | Yes | | | Yes | |
| Spain | Yes | Yes | | Yes | Yes | |
| Sweden | | Yes | Yes | | Yes | |
| Switzerland | | Yes | | | Yes | |
| United Kingdom | | | | Yes | Yes | Yes |

SOURCE: Vernon, J. A., "Drug Research and Price Controls," *Regulation* (Winter 2002/2003).

prices to actual or implied reimbursement rates. Formulary listings can be negotiating tools; if firms will not accept the regulated price, their medicine can be dropped from the list of medicines covered by the regulator. And setting maximum profit rates for firms can effectively cap prices.

These are tactics; they are means to an end. The ultimate goal for most of these countries is to keep pharmaceutical price inflation at or below the average level of consumer price inflation. Indeed,

FIGURE 2-1

COMPARISON OF ANNUAL REAL PHARMACEUTICAL
PRICE INFLATION IN THE UNITED STATES AND THE EU

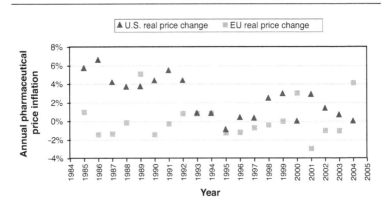

SOURCE: U.S. Bureau of Labor Statistics, Eurostat, and *OECD Health Data.*

when President Clinton proposed pharmaceutical price regulations in 1993, he referred to the goal set by many European countries of zero real pharmaceutical price inflation.

Figure 2-1 shows that the EU countries have indeed attained that goal. Using U.S. Bureau of Labor Statistics, Eurostat, and OECD health data, the figure plots the difference between the annual percentage of change in pharmaceutical prices and the annual percentage of change in the consumer price index, for both the EU and the United States.[1] U.S. prices represent relatively free prices, allowing us to judge the level of price control in the EU. In most of the twenty years between 1985 and 2004, the annual real inflation rate for pharmaceuticals in the EU is close to zero. Cumulative real pharmaceutical inflation over the twenty years is about 4 percent for the EU compared to about 51 percent for the United States. The real inflation rate in the United States exceeds or equals the rate in the EU in all but three years.

Note that the real pharmaceutical inflation rate in the United States dropped sharply in 1993, the year of President Clinton's proposed price regulations to limit the real rate to zero. Ellison and Wolfram (2006) document how U.S. pharmaceutical firms started to moderate their price increases during that period to convince Congress that government price controls were not needed. In fact, since then, U.S. real pharmaceutical price inflation has remained moderate, particularly in the presidential election years of 1996, 2000, and 2004. This illustrates how U.S. pharmaceutical prices are not immune to political threats of price regulation.

Indeed, since 1993, pharmaceutical pricing has become more politicized even though it is not federally regulated. To show that the Clinton plan marked a significant change in how closely the U.S. public (as reflected in the press) watches pharmaceutical price inflation, we searched for articles in the *Wall Street Journal* that discussed average drug price inflation. We found only three articles from 1984 until 1992. But during the period when Clinton developed and proposed price regulations in his Health Security Act (1992–93), twelve such articles appeared. Then, from 1994 through 2005, forty-two articles appeared. Most of these articles focused on the political dimension of the debate.

The U.S. government, as an important buyer of pharmaceuticals, has served to keep a lid on prices even without directly regulating them. The historical evidence is overwhelming that when Uncle Sam enters the picture as buyer, prices are held down. If this influence has been a factor in the past, it will be even more important in the future, especially given the Medicare Modernization Act, which will greatly increase the share of drug purchasing by the U.S. government.

Santerre, Vernon, and Giaccotto (2006) analyze the effect of growing government purchasing on prices. Drawing on extensive databases of actual prices paid, we determined that between 1962 and 2001, every 10 percent rise in the share of government as purchaser of a drug resulted in a 1.2 percent decrease, per year, in prices paid for the drug. In recent years, increased government purchasing has had a much more significant effect. Admittedly, other factors, such as the rise of pharmacy benefit managers (third parties who administer prescription drug programs for insurance companies), have also played a role in capping prices. Yet we estimate that

between 1992 and 2001, a 10 percent increase in government purchasing caused annual real pharmaceutical prices to decrease by
about 5.83 percent. It's important to note that these are price drops
*per year*, so the compounding effect is very large over time.

Looking to the immediate years ahead, pricing pressure on drugs
is bound to accelerate, as Medicare Part D, the Medicare drug-
benefit program, sharply raises the share of drugs paid for by the
U.S. government. Catlin, Cowan, Hartman, and Heffler (2008)
show that the public share of drug spending rose to 36 percent in
2006, up from 28 percent in 2005.

**The Link between Pharmaceutical Prices and R&D Spending**

Not everyone agrees that lower drug prices will trigger drops in
R&D spending. Public Citizen (2001, 2003), Angell (2004), and
Sager and Socolar (2004) suggest that R&D could be unaffected or
even *increase* if drug prices were lower. Their arguments have
amounted at times to mere hostile sentiments toward drug companies: they have suggested that Big Pharma is claiming a drug
price–R&D link in order to mask a strategy of me-too products and
mergers designed to cut competition and expenditures for marketing and advertising (Sager and Socolar 2004).

The fact is, lower prices do affect R&D. And the contrasting
experience of Europe and the United States in R&D spending is clear
evidence that price-limiting policies have huge effects on research.

Public Citizen (2001) claims that EU firms have maintained their
R&D spending despite facing strict price regulation in their home
markets. This is misleading. EU firms' growth in real R&D spending is quite slow compared to U.S. firms' (only 2.8 percent vs. 7.6
percent in recent years [Golec and Vernon 2006]).

Golec and Vernon (2006) show that EU price controls have helped
EU consumers to pay less for pharmaceuticals than U.S. consumers
between 1986 and 2004. But during the same period, the U.S. pharmaceutical industry's R&D spending has grown about twice as fast as
that of the EU. As noted above, in 1986, EU-based pharmaceutical
R&D spending exceeded U.S. spending by about 24 percent ($4,790

million vs. $3,875 million), but by 2004, EU spending trailed U.S. spending by about 15 percent ($26,725 million vs. $30,644 million).

Between 1986 and 2004, EU price controls were increasingly adopted and strengthened. And these years were similarly marked by huge drop-offs in drug research and development. The truly important issue, however, is what the forgone R&D spending in Europe has meant in terms of new drug development. We estimate that reduced R&D from price controls during that period resulted in about fifty fewer new drugs and about seventeen hundred fewer scientists employed in the EU. And whereas EU firms introduced about twice as many new medicines as U.S. firms between 1987 and 1991, they introduced about 20 percent fewer than U.S. firms between 2000 and 2004 (EFPIA 2002, 2005).

To put the issue even more starkly, let's imagine what would have happened to U.S. R&D if the United States had adopted EU-style price controls over the past two decades. The possibilities are disturbing, to say the least. As we pointed out earlier, a regulatory policy that decreases real pharmaceutical prices by 10 percent would likely decrease industry R&D by 6 percent.[2] Using these results and other models (Giaccotto, Santerre, and Vernon 2005), we simulate what would have happened from 1980 to 2004 in the United States if EU-type price controls had limited U.S. pharmaceutical price inflation to average U.S. consumer price inflation. Figure 2-2 illustrates those effects.

First, note that total industry R&D spending is standardized by dividing by industry sales to eliminate the extraneous effects on total dollar sales of such influences as demand increases from population aging. Second, the figure shows that between 1980 and 2001, the U.S. pharmaceutical industry increased the percentage of sales revenue that it devoted to R&D from 9 percent to about 17 percent. Perhaps because of favorable pricing or technology trends, firms were willing to devote more resources to R&D. Under hypothetical price controls, however, the proportion of sales devoted to R&D would have stayed roughly the same, at 9 percent.

Giaccotto, Santerre, and Vernon (2005) use the simulation to calculate how much total R&D spending and how many new

FIGURE 2-2

ACTUAL R&D AS A PERCENTAGE OF SALES COMPARED
TO SIMULATED R&D AS A PERCENTAGE OF SALES ASSUMING
ZERO REAL PHARMACEUTICAL PRICE INFLATION

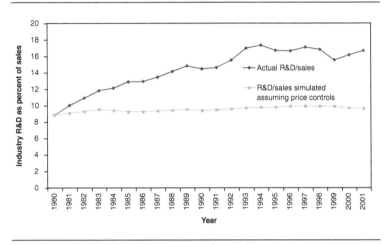

SOURCE: Giaccotto, Santerre, and Vernon, *Journal of Law and Economics*, May 2005.

pharmaceutical introductions would be forgone. They estimate that from 1980 to 2001, between $265 and $293 billion of capitalized R&D expenditures would have been lost. This is about 28 to 31 percent of the actual total capitalized R&D expenditures during the period. Using the estimate of $802 million average R&D cost per new medicine, they calculate that between 330 and 365 new medicines would have gone undeveloped between 1980 and 2001. One cannot be sure whether lifestyle medicines (e.g., Claritin, Nexium, or Viagra) or life-saving drugs (e.g., Avastin, Gleevec, or Epogen) would have been sacrificed; however, price controls could have greater impact on R&D investment decisions for life-saving drugs, because those drugs typically have higher prices.

Ominously, the ill effects associated with price controls have already begun to take hold and to deliver, as theory predicts, less R&D funding into next-generation drugs. Total sales of pharmaceuticals continue to grow as the world population ages and incomes rise.

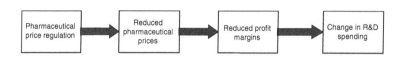

SOURCE: Authors' diagram.

These factors and industry economics should support strong growth in R&D and many new pharmaceuticals. But even U.S. R&D growth is slowing, falling from 9.9 percent between 1981 and 1986, to 7.6 percent between 1999 and 2004.

We believe a significant portion of the R&D spending slowdown is due to tighter pharmaceutical regulations worldwide. Because most firms sell their medicines internationally, they all face price restrictions to some degree. The costs of these restrictions quickly compound into significant forgone R&D spending, and many fewer new medicines.

## The Effects of Pharmaceutical Prices on R&D through Profit Margins

Another approach to testing the relationship between drug price regulation and R&D spending is to focus on an intermediate step between pharmaceutical prices and R&D spending. A number of studies examine how price regulation lowers firm profit margins, i.e., reduces the returns to R&D investment, which in turn reduces a firm's incentive to invest in R&D, at least at the margin. This approach is illustrated in figure 2-3. This formulation gives us a more refined test of the line of causation between price regulation and R&D spending.

The first issue to consider is whether price regulation significantly affects profit margins. Some critics have suggested that pharmaceutical firms can maintain profit margins even with lower regulated prices by

FIGURE 2-4

THE RELATION BETWEEN FIRMS' PROFIT MARGINS
AND SALES VOLUME IN PRICE-REGULATED MARKETS

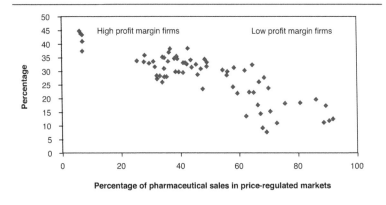

Percentage of pharmaceutical sales in price-regulated markets

SOURCE: Vernon, J. A., "The relationship between price regulation and pharmaceutical profit margins," *Applied Economic Letters* 10: 467–70.

cutting waste, marketing, or other expenses (Angell 2004; Public Citizen 2001). If that were so, why is there such a tight relationship, as we have found, between price levels and profits? In 2003, we examined data from eleven firms, and, estimated each firm's profit margins on sales in price-controlled and free markets respectively (Vernon 2003b). We discovered that the more a firm sells in price-controlled markets, the lower its profit margins, and vice versa. Figure 2-4 illustrates this negative relation.

Some research has taken this analysis a step further and found that internally generated cash is more likely to spur R&D than externally generated funds (such as those gained by floating stock or incurring debt). Vernon (2005) utilizes firm-level profit margin data to estimate models of the determinants of firm R&D investment. This study also includes cash-flow effect to capture the financing advantage of internally generated funds compared to externally generated funds. Results show that price-regulated firms would spend between 23 and 33 percent less on R&D than unregulated firms.

FIGURE 2-5
THE RELATION BETWEEN CAPITAL MARKET FINANCING
AND R&D SPENDING

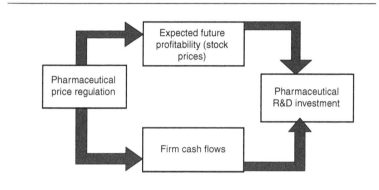

SOURCE: Authors' diagram.

Scherer (2001) documents a close link between gross pharmaceutical profitability and R&D investment at the industry level. The relationship holds tightly, this study suggests, partly because internally generated cash flows from higher sales exert a positive influence on firm R&D spending. Price regulation would negatively affect pharmaceutical profitability and cash flows, and would be expected to reduce industry R&D investment.

### The Effects of Pharmaceutical Prices on R&D through the Capital Market

Many recent studies use firms' stock prices to proxy for expected future profitability. We know from basic finance that firms (and investors) will react immediately to expected future profits. When expected profits are high, stock prices are high, and firms can fund R&D by issuing stock. This is particularly important for the pharmaceutical industry, where firms typically use mostly equity financing. The effects of expected future profitability and current cash flows on R&D are illustrated in figure 2-5.

Lichtenberg (2004) shows that although both current profits and stock prices are related to R&D spending, stock prices do a better job than current profits in explaining R&D. His statistical analysis indicates that stock prices explain more variation in R&D across firms and across time.

Lichtenberg and other scholars have studied how the mere threat of government price controls has sent stock prices spiraling downward, and thereby crimped R&D spending. The premiere case of this threat—and its very real consequences for R&D—came in 1993 with the Health Security Act of the first Clinton administration.

Ellison and Mullin 2001 is an exhaustive "event study" of the sixteen major political events leading up to the day that the Health Security Act was delivered to Congress. An event study measures the stock price changes caused by surprise events. For example, when Clinton leaked his plan to regulate drug prices to the *New York Times*, which reported it on February 16, 1993, pharmaceutical stock prices fell by about 3 percent (after adjustment for the general market return that day). Investors reacted to the new information that price controls could be on the horizon by reducing stock prices.

Ellison and Mullin 2001 finds that eighteen large pharmaceutical company stocks suffered an average 38 percent cumulative loss over all of the Health Security Act events. Golec, Hegde, and Vernon 2008 also finds large negative returns for a wider array of 111 pharmaceutical and biotechnology companies. More important, this study finds that firms that spent proportionately more on R&D suffered larger losses. The top quarter of firms lost 60 percent on average. These firms were mostly small biotechnology firms.

Figure 2-6 shows the stock returns for the market average compared to pharmaceutical stocks grouped by how much they spend on R&D per dollar of their assets (R&D intensity). The start date is January 13, 1992, five trading days before presidential candidate Bill Clinton issued his vague health care white paper. The end date is October 3, 1993, when Hillary Clinton presented the final plan to Congress. The figure shows the severe drop in pharmaceutical firms' stock prices during the period, and makes clear that R&D-intensive firms, many of them biotech firms, suffered the most.

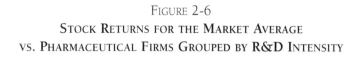

FIGURE 2-6

STOCK RETURNS FOR THE MARKET AVERAGE
VS. PHARMACEUTICAL FIRMS GROUPED BY R&D INTENSITY

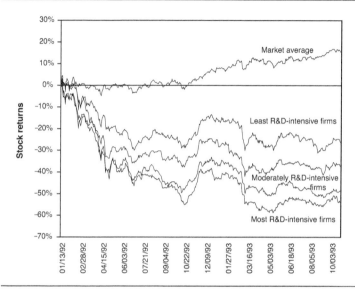

SOURCE: Generated from Center for Research in Securities Prices Database.

The stock market in general did not fall during this period; therefore, one cannot attribute the pharmaceutical industry's stock price declines to general market conditions.

Golec, Hegde, and Vernon (2008) show that the more a firm's stock price fell during this period (which ends in 1993), the more the firm reduced R&D spending in 1994 from what it would have been otherwise. This relation is statistically significant and supports a significant link between the expected net present value of future cash flows (as reflected in stock prices) and R&D spending. Furthermore, because firms' stock prices did not quickly recover when the act did not pass Congress, we know that the threat of future price controls continued to have an effect.

Other event studies have also shown that new government regulations, or threats of regulation, influence firms' share prices. For example, Dowdell, Govindaraj, and Jain (1992) and Dranove and Olsen (1994) show that the introduction of more stringent production, testing, and compliance regulations significantly decreased pharmaceutical firms' stock prices. Although current profits were not affected, investors expected future costs to rise, making pharmaceutical stocks worth less.

Perhaps this is not so surprising, given our understanding of the effects of profit margins and stock prices on R&D spending. Golec and Vernon (2006) show that U.S. firms' profit margins exceeded those of EU firms by an average of five percentage points from 1986 through 2004. And from 1993 to 2004, the percentage return on U.S. pharmaceutical stocks exceeded the return on EU pharmaceutical stocks by 100 percentage points. Relatively high U.S. stock prices have allowed many U.S. biotech firms to raise significant amounts of equity capital to fund R&D spending.

## Bias toward Price Controls for Short-Term Benefits

In the previous section, we noted that because U.S. firms sell more of their medicines at U.S. prices, they have higher profit margins and their investors earn higher returns compared to EU firms. It is no surprise that U.S. firms also increase their R&D more than EU firms. The evidence is clear: free pricing yields higher profit margins, higher stock prices, and more R&D projects. This economic dynamic is very much consistent with the predictions of neoclassical economic theory.

The political dynamic, however, clashes with the economic dynamic. In the next chapter, we will show how pharmaceutical price controls are an easy solution for politicians at a time of rising government budget deficits. That's especially true when neither the public nor the politicians see much immediate connection between price controls and R&D spending.

The issue can be traced, as we have said, to the tension between short-term political agendas and the long-term payoff from pharmaceutical research. The substantial negative effects of price controls appear only after many years, making it difficult to tie the price controls to the R&D effect. But Golec, Hegde, and Vernon (2008) show that negative effects on R&D come even before controls are adopted. Investors discount pharmaceutical firms' share prices as the proba- bility of future price controls increases, and firms start fewer R&D projects because discounted stock finances fewer projects. When price controls are actually adopted, the immediate response in R&D is negative but muted because some of the negative effect has already occurred, and because many current projects will remain profitable under price controls.

We now turn to the rising political clamor to deploy those controls.

# 3

## Government Intervention and the Threats to Drug R&D

In the multibillion dollar market for pharmaceuticals, there are two basic ways that prices can be controlled. One is the marketplace itself. The other is government intervention, by officials who often use complex measures of costs and benefits to rein in drug prices, or who discourage the use of drugs by refusing to pay for them.

The marketplace mostly works quite well, and much the way theory suggests it should. Theoretically, free-market pricing should generate higher prices for breakthrough medicines over incumbent drugs. Lu and Comanor (1998) find that medicines representing important new therapeutic advances are priced between two and three times higher than incumbents. Equally if not more important, me-too medicines or generic versions of breakthrough medicines create a market-based version of price control. They can be cheap to develop and eventually compete with original breakthroughs to keep prices down. Also, new medicines that are therapeutically equivalent to incumbents are priced at the level of incumbents. These results demonstrate that the U.S. market distinguishes between medicines, awarding proportionately higher prices for proportionately more effective medicines.

Outside the United States, however, many governments believe they have found better ways to keep prices under control—by directly tinkering with the market. They think that they have found the drug-pricing equivalent of a free lunch: they establish drug-pricing regimes that provide incentives equal to or better than free-market incentives, but with lower prices on average.

Technology assessment and cost-effectiveness analysis (CEA) are governments' preferred new methods. These largely replace the much cruder government rules of the past, such as insistence on zero real price increases. As we shall see, however, these new tools are fraught with problems. At best, they create profound uncertainties for drug companies, because the firms can't fathom the basis for the rules. At worst, they create for governments more sophisticated weapons to get prices where they want them—low—by manipulating the various assumptions on which their cost-effectiveness analysis is based.

The new techniques have perhaps reached their most sophisticated application in the United Kingdom. Yet, as the ongoing and highly controversial case of the UK's partial ban on Alzheimer's treatments suggests, these new methods of CEA have created a cloud of uncertainty for the makers and marketers of these drugs. That's because the new wave of CEA analysis—the weighing of a drug's costs against its health benefits as measured by its effect on the length or quality of patients' lives—can operate like a bureaucratic black box and serve to confuse and discourage the development of breakthrough drugs.

The National Institute for Clinical Excellence (NICE) in January 2001 decided to fund Alzheimer's disease (AD) drugs under the UK's National Health Service only for patients in the most severe stages of the disease. The decision prompted an immediate backlash from patients and their families, who were suddenly denied their £2.50-per-day reimbursement for several anticholinesterase drugs, including Novartis's Exelon, Shire's Reminyl, and Aricept, a widely prescribed treatment offered by Pfizer Inc. and Japan's Eisai Co. Ltd. (Whalen 2005).

Pfizer and Eisai have led an all-out fight against the NICE decision, arguing that NICE based its denials on a secret cost-benefit formula that it refused to disclose. In May 2008, the drug companies won a round in the legal fight when a British appeals court ruled that NICE had to disclose the computer model of its cost-effectiveness analysis to the drug companies (Jack 2008).

Lack of transparency is hardly the only problem with these emerging new methods. The more basic problem is that of trusting bureaucrats to outperform the markets. To outperform the market, the new methods require bureaucracies to have the resources and incentives to gather the proper information, the technical skills required to interpret the information, and the negotiating skills of specialized intermediaries such as pharmacy benefit managers and health maintenance organizations (HMOs). If this is even possible, it is surely expensive to administer, and we are skeptical that governments will provide enough funding to make it work.

Now let's turn to a more detailed analysis of these new methods for controlling drug prices.

### Current Approaches to Technology Assessment and Cost-Effectiveness Analysis

Various countries with national health plans are trying explicit methods of technology assessment and cost-effectiveness analysis to guide reimbursement and rationing decisions for new pharmaceuticals. Certain health and cost thresholds are set, and if they are not met, the new medicine is excluded from national health plans, just as in the UK the NICE refused to pay for Alzheimer's treatments.

Technology assessment begins with the assumption that market forces are imperfect price setters. Some argue, for instance, that drug companies use their patent protections to extract unseemly prices during the life of the patent, or that patients pay outrageous prices because their insurance companies or employers will actually foot the bill. Many believe the solution is to bring government analysis into the picture. Different analytical formats have been used, including cost-minimization analysis (CMA), cost-benefit analysis (CBA), and cost-effectiveness analysis (Eisenberg 1989).

While CBA has a two-century history in public finance and has several theoretical and practical advantages over CEA, it is seldom used in health care because of the reluctance to attach monetary values to health benefits. In addition, some believe that consumers and providers are too ignorant of new medicines' values, and that this type of analysis does not fit the public payer's budget-level perspective (Sloan 1995).

CEA is more prominent in health care policymaking in some countries because it entails a combination of economic theory, medical information, and empirical flexibility. But CEA still requires someone to assign a monetary value to health benefits. Assigning health benefit value was a contentious issue in the decision to restrict access to AD drugs in the UK. NICE determined that none of four AD drugs it considered met a threshold it had set for health value at their price levels. This threshold criterion can be used as a CEA mechanism for imposing indirect pharmaceutical price controls. Below, we briefly review the CEA method and then demonstrate how it can be used to control prices.

### An Overview of Cost-Effectiveness Analyses

CEA involves comparing the ratio of the difference in marginal costs and benefits between a new therapy and the old or alternative therapy.

$$(1) \quad \frac{\Delta C}{\Delta B} = \frac{NewTherapyCost - AlternativeTherapyCost}{NewTherapyBenefit - AlternativeTherapyBenefit}$$

Costs are generally calculated as the difference between the new drug and the one it replaces. Benefits are measured in standardized units of health such as life years or quality-adjusted life years (QALYs). NICE guidelines, for example, recommend the use of QALYs. It is difficult enough to measure life years—that is, the benefit that occurs when a therapy extends someone's life by one year—but measuring QALYs adds another layer of complexity. QALYs are "weighted" life years. Everyone whose life is extended by one year is not considered equal, and the weight reflects the quality of life in a particular state of health. If a therapy prolongs life but the patient is in poor health during those years, CEA discounts those years. Treatments that improve both the duration and the quality of life get better QALYs (Torrance 1976). Of course, measuring life quality is itself problematic.

Consider the following example of a payer using CEA to evaluate a new therapy which provides an additional life year at a marginal cost of $100,000; that is, the therapy increases costs per patient by

$100,000 over the alternative therapy. For pharmaceuticals, this is reasonably easy to calculate as the difference in medicine prices (and possibly some ancillary costs). Now suppose that the new medicine also increases life years by one and that the payer agrees that an extra year of life is worth $125,000. Then:

$$\frac{\Delta C}{\Delta B} = \frac{\$100,000}{\$125,000} = 0.80$$

A ratio less than 1 ($\Delta C/\Delta B < 1$) implies that the costs are less than the benefits and the medicine would seem to be acceptable. But there are two complications. First, in order to be more confident that the benefits will exceed the costs, the payer could require a smaller ratio—less than 0.50, for example. Second, the payer could decide that this particular life year saved is not worth a full year. Perhaps it is worth only 0.50 years because the patient is an eighty-year-old cancer survivor who will spend his year in a nursing home. Under these conditions we calculate thus:

$$\frac{\Delta C}{\Delta B} = \frac{\$100,000}{(\$125,000)\times 0.5} = 1.60$$

Now, even if the payer only requires the ratio to be less than 1, the new medicine is not acceptable. A thorough CEA requires the payer to consider all alternative medicines. All viable medicines should be compared, and their cost-effectiveness results rank-ordered in a league table. The top medicine or medicines are reimbursed, perhaps at different rates.

A decision to cover and reimburse any of the medicines depends on the payer's willingness to pay, which is implicit in the choice of a ratio cutoff. In our example, we started with a natural cutoff of 1, but different payers can set different cutoffs. If a payer sets the cutoff at 0.50, for instance, far fewer drugs will clear the hurdle. A payer will cover only those medicines with CEA ratios below the cutoff, and will not cover those with ratios above the cutoff.

Determining the cutoff is crucial to the success of CEA used by governments and national payers. The cutoff makes explicit the placement of a monetary value on health benefits. If set too high, almost any new treatment will pass; if set too low, almost none will. In addition, a cutoff set below the true economic value of a health benefit (e.g., a life year) will have the socially undesirable effect of reducing innovation incentives to levels below their socially optimal level. The converse is also true: cutoffs set above the true economic value of a health benefit will encourage too much R&D investment.

Most of Western Europe, Canada, Australia, and New Zealand use explicit or implicit forms of CEA (Jommi 2001; Gosling 2000). The UK's NICE adopted CEA in 1999 to ensure that health care funds are used efficiently, that policies on treatment choice are consistent across the country, and that pharmaceutical products deemed to significantly increase health system expenditures are evaluated for cost-effectiveness (Atkinson 2002).

In the United States, not only Medicare but managed care organizations and state Medicaid programs are considering the possibility of developing formal and informal cost-effectiveness evaluation mechanisms. Even if no explicit CEA system is used, concerns about rising premiums and federal and state budget deficits could cause U.S. payers to consider using CEA.

CEA helps payers to place an explicit value on a new technology. This method can be attractive to payers even if it is imperfect, because it can help convince patients that their health coverage is defined by objective criteria. But it also formally defines a payer's maximum willingness to pay for different pharmaceuticals. Firms can reverse-engineer a maximum price for a medicine when they know how a payer determines its QALYs and its cutoff. Payers may have to reveal QALYs and cutoffs to patients or patient representatives in order to defend their CEA computations. Even if all the details are unknown, firms can use a payer's reimbursement and coverage policies to probabilistically forecast product prices within a given confidence interval.

But one advantage of CEA for firms is that it can reduce the uncertainty in the development or license-acquisition process. CEA essentially sets up a formula that defines the rules of the game. Offer a medicine that passes the cutoff, and product sales are nearly assured. Vernon, Hughen, and Johnson (2005) show how firms have started to make R&D product development and in-licensing decisions based upon the CEA signals being sent by foreign governments via their reimbursement and coverage decisions.[1] The signals to firms may be more reassuring, but they can produce socially suboptimal results if the value payers place on a life year in their budgeting is less than the true economic value of a life year. Research by Murphy and Topel (2003a) on the economic value of a life year suggests national payers are setting their willingness-to-pay thresholds too low.

## Potential Indirect Price Controls: Consequences for R&D Investment

The greatest problem with CEA is that QALYs and cutoffs can be improperly set, discouraging certain R&D projects. A related problem with CEA is that governments can essentially game the system by adjusting the cutoff point, i.e., requiring costs to be so far below expected health benefits that only low-priced drugs survive the cut.

Suppose that the payer sets a cutoff of $K$ and that the cost of a new medicine is its price, $P$. We can rewrite equation (1) as follows.

$$(2) \quad \frac{\Delta C}{\Delta B} = \frac{P - AlternativeTherapyCost}{NewTherapyBenefit - AlternativeTherapyBenefit} = K$$

Now rearrange equation (2) by solving for $P$.

$$(3) \quad P = K * (NewTherapyBenefit - AlternativeTherapyBenefit) - AlternativeTherapyCost$$

Equation (3) shows that a payer can essentially set prices by setting $K$ appropriately, or by defining therapy benefits appropriately. It is reasonable to assume that therapy benefits can vary by disease category. But the payer could even define a separate $K$ for different classes of medicines, arguing that some benefits in some disease categories are more uncertain; hence, these categories would involve a smaller $K$. Given some fixed $K$, defining therapy benefits in a way that makes them appear smaller implicitly reduces $P$. A smaller $K$ also reduces $P$. That is, if the payer measures small benefits or sets $K$ low, only low-price medicines will be reimbursed (all else being equal). Pharmaceutical firms do not need to know the payer's implied $P$; they will rationally interpret the low $K$ or small measured benefit as a signal to avoid starting R&D projects in a particular disease category.

Payers typically announce their choices for $K$ and measurements of benefits. How these are determined (and perhaps who sets them) is therefore critical to implementing CEA in a way that is not equivalent to indirect price controls. So far, the objectivity of some payers is not encouraging. For example, the UK's NICE uses approximately $50,000 per QALY to measure benefits. Research by Hirth, Chernew, and Orzol (2000) and Murphy and Topel (2003a), however, suggests the value of a life year in the United States is much higher, closer to $175,000 in current dollars. These studies estimate QALY values using market data on how much people are willing to pay to avoid hazardous work (and increase their expected life span). Even with a cutoff set at 1, when the UK measures benefits at less than a third of what they may be, fewer pharmaceuticals will pass this criterion.

Some see CEA as essentially a rationing tool, even if it is touted as an improvement over free-market pricing. If CEA is to be adopted in the United States as a rationing device for the Medicare drug benefit, more research and considerable caution are needed. These rationing tools can be as complex and theoretic as policymakers want them to be, but the real question is whether free-market prices send better signals than the rationing tools. We remain skeptical that government rationing tools will perform as well as the free market. Hayek (1945) showed long ago that central planners cannot hope to capture all of the relevant information required to set efficient prices.

Price regulation and price controls in the United States can come in many forms: directly, through prices "negotiated" by the government, and perhaps indirectly, through poorly formulated CEA polices, if CEA is in the U.S. health care system's future. Our concern is that CEA could be used as cover for price controls. Lastly, and very importantly, we see danger in the way the United States is essentially importing the price-control regimes of other countries by allowing large-scale drug importation.

Over the past four years, some U.S. politicians have warmed to drug importation, in part because some economists have argued that it offers a "free lunch"—lower drug prices *and* no harm to drug R&D. A study by Sager and Socolar (2004) in support of drug importation drew a flurry of media attention and was the subject of several press releases by prominent U.S. politicians. The excitement was based on the "finding" that legalized importation of pharmaceuticals from Canada, where prices are regulated by the government, could increase industry profits through higher sales volumes at the lower Canadian prices. Thus, the authors concluded that the industry's intense lobbying effort to defeat legalized importation from Canada (and Europe) was misguided—because importation from Canada could increase its profits.

In U.S. Congressman Rahm Emanuel's (D-IL) press release, issued the same day as the Sager and Socolar press release and report (April 15, 2004), the current chairman of the Democratic Caucus remarked: "This study debunks the profit myth, showing that drug companies can still profit while providing Americans access to lower priced drugs from other countries. . . . Importation is a win-win" (Emanuel 2004). The message was clear: drug companies and their management teams were inept—they couldn't see a good thing when it was directly in front of them. A flurry of legislative initiatives followed, including a Senate importation bill (S.2328), the Pharmaceutical Market Access and Drug Safety Act of 2004.

The claims by Sager and Socolar, parroted by members of Congress, are startling. They assume that pharmaceutical firms' management teams, whose job it is to know pharmaceutical markets, key economic and demographic trends, and product demand, don't in fact know what's best for drug companies. For-profit firms have a fiduciary duty to shareholders to maximize profits. The fact that firms are not pricing their products in the United States at Canadian price levels, and are vehemently opposed to legalized importation, is *prima facie* evidence that such a policy would reduce their profits.[2]

If drug importation is legalized, then rational firm managers, acting on behalf of their shareholders, will divert resources away from pharmaceutical activity and into other, relatively more attractive investment activities. Pharmaceutical R&D will decline. What is uncertain is by how much. As we explained earlier, we believe that if U.S. prices were equivalent to those in price-controlled countries, R&D in the United States would drop by 25 percent to 30 percent.

The debate over these types of polices must recognize and weigh the unavoidable trade-offs and opportunity costs involved. Regulating pharmaceutical prices in the United States, however it might be achieved, will involve forgoing future innovations in order to improve current access to, and lower the cost of, existing medicines. While there is certainly a need for more economic research on the topic, and indeed room for debate, the existing evidence suggests that the trade-off would result in a net social cost to Americans, with future generations bearing a disproportionate share of these costs.

# 4

# Summary and Conclusions:
# Why Public Policy Must Recognize the
# Trade-Off between Lower Prices Today
# and Life-Saving Medicines Tomorrow

In the previous chapters, we made a case against government price controls on drugs. We argued against direct control of prices at launch or at any time after drugs have been marketed. We also argued against indirect forms of price control, whether through cost-effectiveness analysis by government bureaucrats, or mass drug-importation programs sponsored by politicians responding to voter demands. The problem with all this government tinkering is that artificially lowered prices lead to lower revenues and lower profits, and hence to lowered willingness of pharmaceutical companies to keep pursuing the risky, expensive, and time-consuming search for new, breakthrough medicines.

In this concluding chapter, we delve more deeply into the issue that lies beneath the link between drug prices and R&D. Although we've mentioned it earlier, it is worth repeating: there's a trade-off at work here between lower prices today and more breakthrough drugs tomorrow. And unfortunately, all too often, governments and voters choose short-term gains in the form of lower prices, while ignoring the great long-term benefits that flow from temporarily higher prices and profits. Those benefits are the breakthrough drugs that have transformed the treatment of heart disease, slowed or even halted the progress of cancers, and made possible the ongoing effort to unlock the mysteries of Alzheimer's disease and many other intractable illnesses.

There are some reliable generators of increased R&D. They include stronger (or longer) patents and higher profits. Both will increase the economic incentives for R&D and innovation, but will simultaneously reduce access to existing drugs. There are also some reliable generators of a less desirable future, one that features less R&D and less innovation. Price controls and shorter patents (weaker intellectual property rights) will improve access to existing medicines but reduce incentives for R&D and innovation.

This trade-off gives rise to an intergenerational conflict, because the short-term benefits of lower prices help today's citizens in obvious ways, while long-run economic benefits—drugs that cannot be well understood because, for the most part, they don't exist yet—accrue systematically to different generations. For example, there are no significant drugs based upon stem cell science, but resources currently used for stem cell research could produce breakthroughs that benefit mostly future generations.

It's the role of public policy to strike the proper balance between the short term and the long term. Indeed, this balance should be the single most fundamental concern when considering and implementing new government regulations and policies. Regrettably, the long-term consequences of drug price controls are frequently ignored, or their existence denied, by political rhetoric, media sensationalism, and bad economics. Both pharmaceutical industry critics and advocates are guilty of this: some industry critics may deny or ignore the long-run social and economic consequences of a policy, and some industry supporters may ignore or minimize the short-run benefits.

Governments have a powerful incentive to favor the short run: it's cheaper. Favoring the short run will cut budget deficits at a time when the federal budget deficit is large, partly because of new government-sponsored drug benefits. With the new Medicare prescription drug benefit adding many billions more to the U.S. government budget along with Social Security, Medicare, and Medicaid, we suspect that it is only a matter of time before the U.S. government faces a budget crisis. When that time comes, if pharmaceutical price controls are proposed again, we hope that the full list of benefits and costs will be arrayed for the public and policymakers to weigh and compare.

Exacerbating this controversy is the contrast between the market-oriented health care system in the United States and the systems of socialized medicine in Europe, Canada, and elsewhere. These foreign policies are increasingly influential in the United States, as the lower prices abroad create a clamor for large-scale importation of these cheaper drugs.

The debate over drug importation is unlikely to go away. Any consumer can simply look up the price of her medicine at a Canadian pharmaceutical Web site; hence, the benefits to most people are highly tangible. As we argued in the previous chapter, buying drugs from other countries amounts to bringing those countries' price-control regimes to American markets. Rather than being an example of free markets at work, large-scale importation imposes the restrictive, price-controlling regimes of other countries on the United States.

We do not mean to minimize the emotionally charged element in this debate over drug prices. The pharmaceutical industry has an image problem, which has worsened recently. The public's negative perception of the pharmaceutical industry is probably due to two principal factors: (1) the belief that medicine should involve kindness, compassion, and empathy (Green 1995; Flower 1996); and (2) economic illiteracy: the failure of the general public to understand the connection between pricing and the profit incentives to spend on R&D.

Pharmaceutical firms are in the businesses of discovering, developing, marketing, and selling new drugs for a profit; many find this offensive. Politicians, media, special interest groups, and book authors often characterize industry pricing practices with rhetoric such as "unconscionable profiteering" and "price gouging." Consider the titles of three recent books about the pharmaceutical industry: *The Big Fix: How the Pharmaceutical Industry Rips Off American Consumers* (Greider 2003); *Profits Before People: Ethical Standards and the Marketing of Prescription Drugs* (Weber 2006); and *The Truth about the Drug Companies: How They Deceive Us and What to Do about It* (Angell 2004).

Pharmaceutical firms and financial markets, however, fully value the expected dollar "votes" of current and future users of their products. This puts them in conflict with politicians, who largely serve current voters. If future voters could somehow be heard, government policy might be more evenhanded. Unfortunately, drug companies' consideration of future customers doesn't really register with the public, whose animosity is directed at Big Pharma. This is especially unfortunate considering that price controls will create the biggest disincentives in smaller and more innovative firms, which for many years have taken some of the biggest R&D risks, engaging in early-stage research without the infrastructure or financial stability of the bigger firms.

Chapter 2 showed that the mere threat of price controls drove pharmaceutical stock prices down significantly, with the largest declines suffered by R&D-intensive firms. These firms also happen to be the smaller, younger, innovative firms with little sales revenue and mostly early-stage R&D projects. A number of simulation models predict that, indeed, the firms most likely to be severely affected by price controls are the early-stage firms. These studies include Abbott and Vernon 2007, Filson and Masia 2007, and Vernon 2003c. They use evolutionary economic models of value-maximizing firms of various sizes and characteristics to simulate the effect of price controls on the structure of the industry. The large firms, which are more harshly criticized in the popular press and by citizens' action groups, have established products that help them limit the damage. They have the resources to adapt to the new regulated environment. Conversely, the studies show that the small early-stage firms often die off under price controls. This leaves a less healthy competitive environment because new innovative firms have less chance of start-up and survival, and large firms have less to fear from innovative upstarts.

Furthermore, Higgins and Rodriguez (2006) show that successful small firms are likely to be bought out by the large ones to fill their R&D pipelines. This strategy essentially outsources the uncertain R&D function, leaving small firms to bear the risk. Because price regulation reduces the payoff for risk taking, this is a rational strategy for large firms.

These effects do not create much of a political counterweight against regulation, because the decline of small innovative firms does not happen immediately. Like the decline in innovative activity in the EU's pharmaceutical industry, the effects of price controls are not observed immediately; rather, they accumulate over time. Pharmaceutical R&D projects take fifteen years on average to bear fruit, and because most late-stage projects are still worthwhile even under price controls (their costs are already sunk), new products will continue to enter the market, albeit at a progressively slower rate. This makes it difficult for consumers and policymakers to tie the regulatory policy to its negative effects.

Benefits to consumers, however, are immediate and tangible. This produces an unfortunate political dynamic in which price-control policies yield immediate gains without showing immediate large costs. This could vindicate politicians' price-control policies, garnering them votes and reelection. The major costs come well after they leave office.

Pharmaceutical price regulation is also not good news for generic drug companies. Danzon and Chao (2000b) show that price regulation undermines price competition generated by generic firms. Therefore, if price regulations are adopted in the United States, one can expect fewer generic firms to survive and the remaining generic firms to become weaker competitors—that is, to charge higher prices. Indeed, Graham (2001) shows that in price-regulated Canada, generic pharmaceuticals sell for more than they do in the United States. Part of the reason that U.S. generics are less expensive is that entry into the U.S. market by generic firms has been eased since 1984, producing a strong, competitive generic market (see Grabowski and Vernon 1992). Furthermore, Danzon and Chao (2000a) show that the United States consumes proportionately more generic pharmaceuticals than most price-regulated countries. Hence, when properly weighted by the amounts consumed, average U.S. pharmaceutical prices are much closer to regulated-market prices than is typically assumed.

Many public action groups ask why pharmaceutical firms' productivity has declined; why firms produce so many me-too medicines; why they pay so much to market their products; why so few new vaccines or AIDS medicines are produced; and why so many life-style medicines are produced. Behind each question is a suspicion of sinister intent on the part of large, profitable pharmaceutical firms. In truth, no one can be sure about the correct answers to each question.

This is the beauty of a free market. Firms, and the industry as a whole, are molded by their economic environment and respond to its incentives. Left to their own, most free markets are driven to produce the product consumers demand, at the best price. But poor or convoluted incentives can lead to poor outcomes, and the evidence shows that price controls for pharmaceuticals provide poor incentives. Why produce high-R&D breakthrough medicines when commensurate high prices are not allowed? Given the price controls that pharmaceutical firms face in most countries, and could soon face in the United States, what looks like "sinister" behavior to some may simply be an optimal response to misguided policy incentives.

.

# Appendix
# National Survey on Public Perceptions of the Pharmaceutical Industry and Economic Illiteracy

To gauge the prevalence of economic illiteracy among the general public with respect to the pharmaceutical industry, and to measure general public perception of the industry, we conducted a random national telephone survey. The survey questions were designed, and the polling was undertaken, in 2005. We obtained responses from 1,006 randomly selected Americans. Our results have not previously been published.[1]

We intended to measure the public's most basic understanding of the pharmaceutical industry. For example, we asked questions about whether the elimination of intellectual property rights and patents would affect drug companies' incentives for doing research. We also asked whether price controls would affect R&D spending. There were also numerous questions about people's impressions of drug research, the value of new pharmaceuticals, drug prices, and profits, etc.

We report only some of these results in this appendix (those most germane to the direct questions of economic literacy and public perception). We collected demographic data that revealed how different groups responded to the survey questions, but we report only aggregate survey responses here to give a broad overview of the public's understanding of the economics of intellectual property rights and their general views of the industry as a whole. Full survey results are obtainable from the authors.

One question we asked concerned the importance of patents as a means to incentivize research. After a brief description of what pharmaceutical patents are, and why they are important, we read the following question to survey subjects.

**Question 1:** *Do you think that pharmaceutical or drug companies would continue to do research and development for new drugs if they were not able to have these patents?*

The survey responses to this question are summarized in table A-1.

Another question we asked, one particularly germane to the discussion and examples of economic illiteracy previously covered, concerned the effect that pharmaceutical price controls in the United States might have on future R&D spending.

**Question 2:** *Suppose the government controlled the prices of prescription drugs. Do you think that pharmaceutical or drug companies would spend more, less, or about the same amount on scientific research to find new drugs?*

We found that a significant fraction of the general public is misinformed or confused when it comes to the economic realities of this issue. Perhaps this should not be surprising when high-profile economists, such as former FDA commissioner Mark McClellan, are harshly criticized for even suggesting that price controls might discourage incentives for R&D. Table A-2 summarizes the responses to this question.

In a related question, we asked whether importing drugs from Canada, where the government controls pharmaceutical prices, would have an effect on drug companies' R&D spending. The additional layer of complexity (importing price-regulated drugs versus direct U.S. price controls) resulted in a higher proportion of responders believing that R&D would not be affected. We asked subjects the following question.

**Question 3:** *Some people say that allowing Americans to buy prescription drugs imported from Canada will lead United States pharmaceutical*

TABLE A-1
**WOULD PHARMACEUTICAL R&D CONTINUE WITHOUT PATENTS?**

| Survey response | Percent of responses |
|-----------------|----------------------|
| Yes             | 39                   |
| No              | 52                   |
| Don't know      | 8                    |
| Refused         | 0                    |
| **Total count** | **100**              |

TABLE A-2
**HOW WOULD U.S. PRICE CONTROLS INFLUENCE R&D SPENDING?**

| Survey response | Percent of responses |
|-----------------|----------------------|
| Spend more      | 15                   |
| Spend less      | 42                   |
| Spend the same  | 40                   |
| Don't know      | 3                    |
| Refused         | 0                    |
| **Total count** | **100**              |

*or drug companies to do less research and development. Do you agree or disagree?*

The distribution of responses to this question is presented in table A-3.

These results may partially explain why importation, as a political strategy to control U.S. drug prices, has been more successful in Congress than more direct efforts. This is the case despite the additional concerns over drug importation safety. Over 70 percent of people surveyed did not see importation as a threat to firm R&D. This is compared to 55 percent of survey respondents who believed that direct government price controls in the United States would not be a threat, or might actually act as a stimulus for more R&D. It is possible that this difference is due to uncertainty about how an

TABLE A-3
WILL PHARMACEUTICAL IMPORTATION DECREASE R&D?

| Survey response | Percent of responses |
|---|---|
| Strongly agree | 11 |
| Somewhat agree | 15 |
| Somewhat disagree | 23 |
| Strongly disagree | 48 |
| Don't know | 2 |
| Refused | 0 |
| **Total count** | **100** |

importation policy might be implemented, to increased pressure on foreign governments to set prices differently, or to judgments about the eventual scale and volume of importation.

We also asked a series of questions that were intended to shed light on the public image of the pharmaceutical industry and to learn the public's opinions about pharmaceutical prices and profits as well as the value of pharmaceuticals and pharmaceutical R&D. These questions and answers are presented next.[2]

**Question 4:** *Would you say that prescription drugs are priced fairly or unfairly?*

**Question 5:** *Do you think that the profits pharmaceutical or drug companies make are too high, too low, or about right?*

Note that out of approximately a thousand randomly questioned Americans, not a single person thought pharmaceutical profits were too low. This by itself is not terribly surprising. What is intriguing is research by Kevin M. Murphy, Robert H. Topel, and other prominent economists suggesting that the United States may be investing too little in medical and pharmaceutical research (Murphy and Topel 2003a, 2003b). The economic benefits of increasing investment in medical research, through gains in life expectancy and good health, may be substantially greater than the cost of the research

TABLE A-4
ARE DRUGS PRICED FAIRLY OR UNFAIRLY?

| Survey response | Percent of responses |
|---|---|
| Fairly | 12 |
| Unfairly | 77 |
| Depends | 3 |
| Don't know | 7 |
| Refused | 0 |
| **Total count** | **100** |

TABLE A-5
OPINION OF DRUG COMPANY PROFITS

| Survey response | Percent of responses |
|---|---|
| Too high | 70 |
| Too low | 0 |
| About right | 21 |
| Don't know | 9 |
| Refused | 0 |
| **Total count** | **100** |

itself. Studies by Frank Lichtenberg (2002, 2005, 2007) have repeatedly suggested that the same is true for pharmaceutical R&D, at least historically. If this is true, then pharmaceutical profits may be "too low" because profits, and more specifically expected future profits, are what attract investment dollars into R&D.[3]

To probe the issue of pharmaceutical profits a little deeper, we also asked the following question, which consisted of three parts asked in a random order.

**Question 6:** *Sometimes when people find out new information they change their opinion and sometimes they don't. I'm going to read you a list of items. After you hear each, please tell me if you think that the* *profits pharmaceutical or drug companies make are too high, too low, or about right.*

*a) Drug companies earned about average profits compared to other brand-name companies of their size. Knowing this, please tell me if you think that the profits pharmaceutical or drug companies make are too high, too low, or about right.*

*b) Some drugs have actually lowered the overall cost of care by reducing hospital stays or invasive treatment. Knowing this, please tell me if you think that the profits pharmaceutical or drug companies make are too high, too low, or about right.*

*c) Lower prices today might mean that fewer new drugs are available in the future. Knowing this, please tell me if you think that the profits pharmaceutical or drug companies make are too high, too low, or about right.*

Presenting survey respondents with qualifying statements on the pharmaceutical industry's profits relative to other U.S. industries, on the effect of drugs on overall health care costs, and on the trade-off between access to existing drugs and innovation in the future had only a moderate effect on their perceptions of profit levels in the pharmaceutical industry. This may simply reflect prior knowledge of the information provided, but given the responses to some of the earlier questions, it appears that the public's opinions about pharmaceutical firms' profits do not change even in light of new information.

The next question addressed the trade-off between short- and long-run economic benefits of pharmaceutical technology (albeit in a very blunt and imprecise manner). As is always the case with survey research, different respondents may have different interpretations of the question being asked. Nevertheless, the question has value in that it indirectly addresses whether the public recognizes the opportunity costs involved in trading short- and long-run economic benefits.

**Question 7:** *Is it more important for pharmaceutical or drug companies to lower the cost of the drugs they have already developed, or to continue to do research on new drugs for the future?*

TABLE A-6a
OPINION OF DRUG COMPANY PROFITS—QUALIFIED
("PROFITS ARE AVERAGE")

| Survey response | Percent of responses |
| --- | --- |
| Too high | 54 |
| Too low | 2 |
| About right | 39 |
| Don't know | 4 |
| Refused | 0 |
| Total count | 100 |

TABLE A-6b
OPINION OF DRUG COMPANY PROFITS—QUALIFIED
("DRUGS LOWER COST OF CARE")

| Survey response | Percent of responses |
| --- | --- |
| Too high | 49 |
| Too low | 3 |
| About right | 43 |
| Don't know | 4 |
| Refused | 1 |
| Total count | 100 |

TABLE A-6c
OPINION OF DRUG COMPANY PROFITS—QUALIFIED
("LOWER DRUG PRICES MEAN FEWER NEW DRUGS")

| Survey response | Percent of responses |
| --- | --- |
| Too high | 52 |
| Too low | 4 |
| About right | 39 |
| Don't know | 4 |
| Refused | 1 |
| Total count | 100 |

TABLE A-7
SHOULD DRUG COMPANIES LOWER COSTS
OR CONTINUE RESEARCH?

| Survey response | Percent of responses |
|---|---|
| Lower costs | 36 |
| Continue research | 55 |
| Don't know | 7 |
| Refused | 2 |
| **Total count** | **100** |

The results in table A-7, which indicate that the public values new drugs in the future over lower costs today, are difficult to reconcile with those presented in table A-6c, which indicate that the public values lower costs today over new drugs in the future. Perhaps, as discussed earlier, the discrepancy can be explained by the negative connotation associated with profits in medicine. Question 7 addresses the trade-off between access and innovation without mentioning the intermediate role played by profits. Question 6c addresses profitability directly. As already noted, it may also simply be a reflection of how the question was interpreted; Question 7 may have been interpreted as a binary choice between lower drug prices and new research.

The final two survey questions for which we will present results dealt with overall impressions of the industry and with opinions about the contribution and value of pharmaceutical research and new drug innovation.

**Question 8:** *Do you have a favorable or an unfavorable opinion of pharmaceutical or drug companies that make prescription drugs?*

**Question 9:** *How important of a contribution do pharmaceutical or drug companies make by researching and developing new drugs and treatments?*

The last two questions seem to show that respondents recognize the value and importance of pharmaceutical research and innovation,

TABLE A-8
OPINION OF PHARMACEUTICAL FIRMS

| Survey response | Percent of responses |
| --- | --- |
| Strongly favorable | 14 |
| Somewhat favorable | 32 |
| Somewhat unfavorable | 21 |
| Strongly unfavorable | 19 |
| Don't know | 13 |
| Refused | 1 |
| **Total count** | **100** |

TABLE A-9
IMPORTANCE OF PHARMACEUTICAL FIRMS' RESEARCH
AND INNOVATION

| Survey response | Percent of responses |
| --- | --- |
| Very important | 59 |
| Somewhat important | 36 |
| Not too important | 2 |
| Not at all important | 2 |
| Don't know | 1 |
| Refused | 0 |
| **Total count** | **100** |

but this favorable view of the activity does not translate into approval of such research. We suspect that this is due to the motivation underlying the research: profits.

# Notes

## Introduction

1. See the appendix for the results of our survey, previously unpublished.

2. Golec and Vernon (2006) compute these figures based upon data supplied by European Federation of Pharmaceutical Industries and Associations (EFPIA) for Europe and Pharmaceutical Researchers and Manufacturers of America (PhRMA) for the United States. Members of both organizations supply separate R&D figures for the United States and Europe. For example, Pfizer might report $2 billion R&D spending in the United States and $1 billion in Europe. The next year, if Pfizer relocates a U.S. R&D facility to Europe, it might report $1.5 billion of R&D in the United States and $1.5 billion in Europe.

## Chapter 1: R&D Investment in New Drugs: How It Works, and How It Is Harmed by Price Controls

1. We denote the time of the Phase I "go/no-go" decision as $t = 0$. A profit-maximizing firm decides whether or not to extend an R&D project into Phase I clinical development as follows. Defining period $t$ expected cash flows (negative values during drug development and positive values after launch) as $E(C_t)$, an R&D project with final-year product sales in period $T$ will have the following expected NPV:

$$(1) \quad E(NPV_0) = \sum_{t=0}^{T} \frac{E(C_t)}{(1+r)^t} = E(C_0) + \frac{E(C_1)}{(1+r)^1} + \frac{E(C_2)}{(1+r)^2} + \frac{E(C_3)}{(1+r)^3} + \dots + \frac{E(C_T)}{(1+r)^T}$$

The discount rate $r$ in equation (1) is the firm's cost of capital and is assumed to be constant. Profit-maximizing firms will take the R&D project into Phase I clinical development if $E(NPV_0) > 0$; they will terminate the project, however, if $E(NPV_0) < 0$. The project's expected internal rate of return, which we will discuss later in the chapter, is the value of $r$ that results in $E(NPV_0) = 0$.

2. We made this point in testimony before the Senate Commerce, Science, and Transportation Committee (John A. Vernon: Hearing on the Policy Implications of Pharmaceutical Importation for U.S. Consumers) in March 2007 (http://commerce.senate.gov/public/index.cfm?FuseAction=Hearings.Hearing&Hearing_ID=777fd1ca-1393-45dd-a60b-0b46ee444fe3).

3. It is easier to understand why the general public—unfamiliar with some of the economic and regulatory nuances of the pharmaceutical industry—fails to recognize the opportunity costs and trade-offs associated with new public policies. New pharmaceuticals are essentially information products, much like computer software; as such, they require intellectual property rights in the form of limited-term patents to establish economic incentives for their discovery and development. Once a new molecular structure has been discovered and studied in clinical trials, to ensure it is both safe and effective in humans (a process that takes over a decade and may cost over $1 billion), the final result is essentially a massive dossier of clinical, pharmacological, and scientific information. Generic pharmaceutical markets in the United States are highly competitive for this reason, with prices being rapidly driven down to marginal costs (Saha, Grabowski, et al. 2006). The United States, unlike other countries, greatly facilitates competition in generic pharmaceutical markets and does not regulate its drug prices. As a result, Americans enjoy the lowest-priced generic drugs in the world.

## Chapter 2: Government Price Regulation and the Impact on Pharmaceutical R&D Spending

1. U.S. pharmaceutical and CPI (all items price 1982–84 = 100) indexes are from the Bureau of Labor Statistics (www.bls.gov/cpi/home.htm#data). EU CPI is from Eurostat Harmonized Indices of Consumer Prices (all items) (epp.eurostat.ec.europa.eu/portal/page?_pageid=1090,30070682,1090_33076576&_dad=portal&_schema=PORTAL). The EU pharmaceutical price index is from Eurostat starting in 2001 and compiled from *OECD Health Data 2003* for the years before 2001.

2. Using different data, Lichtenberg (2007) estimates a similar size relation.

## Chapter 3: Government Intervention and the Threats to Drug R&D

1. Vernon, Hughen, and Johnson (2005) describe the various methods used within this context by firm managers, especially for potential projects in the earliest stages of drug development.

2. Empirical research has also consistently revealed that the demand for pharmaceuticals is inelastic. See Coulson and Stuart 1995; Pauly 2004; Santerre and Vernon 2006.

## Appendix: National Survey on Public Perceptions of the Pharmaceutical Industry and Economic Illiteracy

1. The University of Connecticut's Roper Center for Public Opinion Research conducted the survey on behalf of the authors.

2. Additional questions relating to direct-to-consumer advertising, insurance, and drug consumption and expenditures were also asked, but these questions are beyond the scope of this appendix.

3. Of course this possibility is not easily communicated because of the economic illiteracy surrounding the process by which R&D investment decisions are made (the subject of chapter 2). The following exchange between Joseph DiMasi, professor, Tufts Center for the Study of Drug Development, and Donald W. Light, professor, University of Medicine and Dentistry of New Jersey, in a series of recent *Health Affairs* eLetters demonstrates this point and the challenge to overcoming economic illiteracy (so the right questions and issues can be debated). Joseph DiMasi had asserted that "expected R&D (and other) costs [of developing new drugs] together with expected prices (and associated quantities demanded) determine expected profitability. Expected profitability, in turn, determines the incentive to develop new therapies." DiMasi is just saying what economists have known and been saying for over a century. Yet Light denies DiMasi's seemingly unobjectionable claim: "DiMasi asserts that expected R&D costs, prices, and demand determine expected profitability. No, they don't. How can an expected something, minus an expected something else, be said to determine anything?" (*Health Affairs* 2006). How about the price of a share of Pfizer stock? Expectations are the cornerstone of economic theory; Robert Lucas won a Nobel Prize in 1995 for his work on rational expectations. In the same letter, Light suggests that his exchange with DiMasi "would make good material for classroom discussion about pharmaceutical policy and argumentation." Indeed it would, but in an economics class.

# References

Abbott, Thomas A. and John A. Vernon. 2007. The cost of U.S. pharmaceutical price regulation: A financial simulation model of R&D decisions. *Managerial and Decision Economics* 28: 293–306.

Angell, Marcia. 2004. *The Truth about the Drug Companies: How They Deceive Us and What to Do about It.* New York: Random House Publishing Group.

Atkinson, Sarah. 2002. Political cultures, health systems, and health policy. *Social Science & Medicine* 55: 113–24.

Berenson, Alex and Andrew Pollack. 2007. Doctors reaping millions for use of anemia drugs. *New York Times*, May 9, 1.

Catlin, Aaron, Cathy Cowan, Micah Hartman, and Stephen Heffler. 2008. National health spending in 2006: A year of change for prescription drugs. *Health Affairs* 27: 14–29.

Chase, Marilyn. 2007. Boss talk: How Genentech wins at blockbuster drugs—CEO to critics of prices: 'Give Me a Break.' *Wall Street Journal*, June 5, B1.

Coulson, N. E. and B. C. Stuart. 1995. Insurance choice and the demand for prescription drugs. *Southern Economic Journal* 61: 1146–57.

Danzon, Patricia, Y. Richard Wang, and Liang Wang. 2003. The impact of price regulation on the launch delay of new drugs. National Bureau of Economic Research Working Paper No. 9874.

Danzon, Patricia M. and Li-Wei Chao. 2000a. Cross-national price differences for pharmaceuticals: How large and why? *Journal of Health Economics* 19:159–74.

————. 2000b. Does regulation drive out competition in pharmaceutical markets? *Journal of Law and Economics* 43: 311–57.

DiMasi, Joseph A., Ronald W. Hansen, and Henry G. Grabowski. 2003. The price of innovation: New estimates of drug development costs. *Journal of Health Economics* 22: 151–85.

Dowdell, Thomas D., Suresh Govindaraj, and Prem C. Jain. 1992. The Tylenol incident, ensuing regulation, and stock prices. *Journal of Financial and Quantitative Analysis* 27: 283–302.

Dranove, David and Chris Olsen. 1994. The economic side effects of dangerous drug announcements. *Journal of Law and Economics* 37: 323–49.

Eisenberg, J. M. 1989. A guide to the economic analysis of clinical practices. *Journal of the American Medical Association* 262: 2879–86.

Ellison, Sara Fisher and Wallace P. Mullin. 2001. Gradual incorporation of information: Pharmaceutical stocks and the evolution of President Clinton's health care reform. *Journal of Law and Economics* 44: 89–130.

Ellison, Sara Fisher and Catherine Wolfram. 2006. Coordinating on lower prices: pharmaceutical pricing under political pressure. *Rand Journal of Economics* 37: 324–41.

Emanuel, Rahm. 2004. Press release. Members comment on study showing importation efforts will help Americans afford Rx drugs, may actually increase drug company profits. Washington, D.C., April 15. http://www.house.gov/apps/list/speech/il05_emanuel/stmt_boston_univ_rx_study.html (accessed October 15, 2008).

European Federation of Pharmaceutical Industries and Associations (EFPIA). 2002. *Year in Review 2001–2002*. Brussels: EFPIA.

_____. 2005. *The Pharmaceutical Industry in Figures*. Brussels: EFPIA.

Eurostat, epp.eurostat.ec.europa.eu/portal/page?_pageid=1090,30070682,1090_33076576&_dad=portal&_schema=PORTAL (accessed October 15, 2008).

Filson, Darren and Neal Masia. 2007. Effects of profit-reducing policies on firm survival, financial performance, and new drug introductions in the research-based pharmaceutical industry. *Managerial and Decision Economics* 28, no. 4-5: 329–51.

Flower, Joe. 1996. For profit. Not for profit. Good. Evil. Proprietary. Mission-driven. Evil. Good. Investor-owned. Non-profit. *Healthcare Forum Journal* 39: 26–35.

Giaccotto, Carmelo, Rexford Santerre, and John A. Vernon. 2005. Drug prices and research and development investment behavior in the pharmaceutical industry. *Journal of Law and Economics* 48: 195–214.

Golec, Joseph, Shantaram Hegde, and John A. Vernon. 2008. Pharmaceutical R&D spending and threats of price regulation. Forthcoming in *Journal of Financial and Quantitative Analysis*.

Golec, Joseph and John A. Vernon. 2006. European pharmaceutical price regulation, firm profitability, and R&D spending. National Bureau of Economic Research Working Paper No. 12676.

Gosling, Hugh. 2000. Pharmacoeconomics in Europe: The fourth hurdle. *Global Pharmaceutical Reports*. SMi Publishing, www.smi-online.co.uk/reports/overview.asp?is=4&ref=998 (accessed October 15, 2008).

Grabowski, Henry G. and John M. Vernon. 1992. Brand loyalty, entry, and price competition in pharmaceuticals after the 1984 drug act. *Journal of Law and Economics* 35: 331–50.

Grabowski, Henry G., John M. Vernon, and Joseph DiMasi. 2002. Returns on research and development for 1990s new drug introductions. *PharmacoEconomics* 20, supplement 3: 11–29.

Graham, Robert R. 2001. Seeing through the snow. *Regulation* 24: 46–49.

Green, Michael. 1995. What (if anything) is wrong with residency overwork? *Annals of Internal Medicine* 123, no. 7: 512–17.

Greider, Katharine. 2003. *The Big Fix: How the Pharmaceutical Industry Rips Off American Consumers.* New York: Public Affairs.

Hayek, Friedrich. 1945. The use of knowledge in society. *American Economic Review* 35: 519–30.

*Health Affairs.* 2006. The real significance of development times. eLetters. http://content.healthaffairs.org/cgi/eletters/25/2/461 (accessed October 15, 2008).

Higgins, Matthew J. and Daniel Rodriguez. 2006. The outsourcing of R&D through acquisitions in the pharmaceutical industry. *Journal of Financial Economics* 80: 351–83.

Hirth, R. A., M. E. Chernew, and S. M. Orzol. 2000. Ownership, competition, and the adoption of new technologies and cost-saving practices in a fixed-price environment. *Inquiry* 37: 282–94.

Jack, Andrew. 2008. Drug groups win Alzheimer's appeal. *Financial Times,* May 2, 4.

Jommi, C. 2001. *Pharmaceutical Policy and Organization of the Regulatory Authorities in the Main EU Countries.* Milan: Egea Publishing.

Lichtenberg, Frank R. 2002. Benefits and costs of newer drugs: An update. *Managerial and Decision Economics* 28: 485–90.

———. 2004. Public policy and innovation in the U.S. pharmaceutical industry. In *Public Policy and the Economics of Entrepreneurship.* Eds. Douglas Holtz-Eakin and Harvey S. Rosen. Cambridge: MIT Press, 83–114.

———. 2005. The impact of new drug launches on longevity: Evidence from longitudinal disease-level data from 52 countries, 1982–2001. *International Journal of Health Care Finance and Economics* 5: 47–73.

———. 2007. Importation and innovation. *Economics of Innovation and New Technology* 16: 403–17.

Lu, John and William S. Comanor. 1998. Strategic pricing of new pharmaceuticals. *Review of Economics and Statistics* 80: 108–18.

Miller, Wilhemine, Lisa A. Robinson, and Robert S. Lawrence, eds. 2006. *Valuing Health for Regulatory Cost-Effectiveness Analysis.* Washington, D.C.: National Academies Press.

Murphy, Kevin M. and Robert H. Topel. 2003a. The economic value of medical research. In *Measuring the Gains from Medical Research: An Economic Approach.* Eds. Kevin M. Murphy and Robert H. Topel. Chicago: University of Chicago Press, 41–73.

Murphy, Kevin M. and Robert H. Topel, eds. 2003b. *Measuring the Gains from Medical Research: An Economic Approach.* Chicago: University of Chicago Press.

Neumann P. J., A. B. Rosen, and M. C. Weinstein. 2005. Medicare and cost-effectiveness analysis. *New England Journal of Medicine* 353: 1516–22.

Organisation for Economic Co-operation and Development. 2003. *OECD Health Data 2003: A Comparative Analysis of 30 Countries.* OECD Publishing, Paris.

Pauly, M. 2004. Medicare drug coverage and moral hazard. *Health Affairs* 23: 113–122.

Public Citizen. 2001. *Rx R&D Myths: The Case Against the Drug Industry's R&D Scare Card.* Washington, D.C.: Public Citizen Congress Watch.

———. 2003. *America's Other Drug Problem. A Briefing Book on the Rx Drug Debate.* Washington, D.C.: Public Citizen Congress Watch.

Sager, Alan and Deborah Socolar. 2004. Do drug makers make money on Canadian imports? Boston University School of Public Health. Data Brief No. 6.

Saha, Atanu, Henry Grabowski, Howard Birnbaum, Paul Greenberg, and Oded Bizan. 2006. Generic competition in the U.S. pharmaceutical industry. *International Journal of the Economics of Business* 13: 15–38.

Santerre, Rexford E., John A. Vernon, and Carmelo Giaccotto. 2006. The impact of indirect government controls on U.S. drug prices and R&D. *Cato Journal* 26: 143–58.

Santerre, Rexford E. and John A. Vernon. 2006. Assessing the gains from a drug price control policy in the U.S.. *Southern Economic Journal* 73: 233–45.

Scherer, F. M. 2001. The link between gross profitability and pharmaceutical R&D spending. *Health Affairs* 20: 216–20.

Sloan, Frank, ed. 1995. *Valuing Health Care: Costs, Benefits, and Effectiveness of Pharmaceuticals and Other Medical Technologies.* Cambridge: Cambridge University Press.

Torrance, G. W. 1976. Social preferences for health states: An empirical evaluation of three measurement techniques. *Socio-Economic Planning Sciences* 10: 129–36.

U.S. Bureau of Labor Statistics, www.bls.gov/cpi/home.htm#data.

Vernon, John A.. 2003a. Drug research and price controls. *Regulation* 23: 22–25.

⸻. 2003b. The relationship between price regulation and pharmaceutical profit margins. *Applied Economic Letters* 10: 467–70.

⸻. 2003c. Simulating the impact of price regulation on pharmaceutical innovation, *Pharmaceutical Development and Regulation* 1: 55–65.

⸻. 2005. Examining the link between price regulation and pharmaceutical R&D investment. *Health Economics* 14: 1–16.

Vernon, John A., W. Keener Hughen, and Scott J. Johnson. 2005. Mathematical modeling and pharmaceutical pricing: Analyses used to inform in-licensing and developmental go/no-go decisions. *Health Care Management Science* 8: 167–79.

Weber, L. J. 2006. *Profits Before People: Ethical Standards and the Marketing of Prescription Drugs.* Bloomington, IN: University of Indiana Press.

Whelan, Jeanne. 2005. Valued lives: Britain stirs outcry by weighing benefits of drugs versus prices. *Wall Street Journal*, November 22, A1.

# About the Authors

**John A. Vernon** is a professor in the Department of Health Policy and Management at the University of North Carolina at Chapel Hill, where he also holds appointments in the Kenan-Flagler Business School and the UNC School of Pharmacy. Prior to joining the faculty at UNC, he was a professor in the Finance Department in the School of Business at the University of Connecticut and a visiting professor at the Wharton School of Business at the University of Pennsylvania. He is the former senior economic policy advisor to the Office of the Commissioner at the U.S. Food and Drug Administration and is a Faculty Research Fellow with the National Bureau of Economic Research. He has twice testified before the United States Senate on issues related to the economics of pharmaceutical price regulation. His research has appeared in such journals as the *Journal of Law and Economics*, the *Journal of Financial and Quantitative Analysis*, the *International Journal of Healthcare Finance and Economics*, *Health Economics*, *Inquiry,* the *Southern Economic Journal*, and *Regulation*. He recently guest-edited a special issue of the journal *Managerial and Decision Economics* devoted to the economics of the pharmaceutical industry. Vernon frequently advises both government and industry on a broad range of issues affecting the pharmaceutical industry.

**Joseph H. Golec** is an associate professor of finance at the University of Connecticut. He received his BA in economics from Trinity College in Hartford, Connecticut. He earned an MA and PhD in financial economics from Washington University in St. Louis, Missouri. After teaching finance at Clark University in Worcester, Massachusetts, he joined the Finance Department at the University of

Connecticut in 2000. He teaches investments, finance theory, and health care finance. His research looks at investments, mutual funds, and health care/pharmaceutical finance. Most recently he has examined how pharmaceutical and biotechnology R&D is affected by reimportation, European price controls, threats of U.S. price controls, and follow-on biologics.

www.ingramcontent.com/pod-product-compliance
Lightning Source LLC
Jackson TN
JSHW080854211224
75817JS00002B/41